FELT BOARD
FINGERPLAYS

Favorite Fingerplays Come Alive

FELT BOARD
FINGERPLAYS

by
Liz & Dick Wilmes

Illustrations by
Janet McDonnell

A  Publication

38W567 Brindlewood, Elgin, Illinois 60123

ACKNOWLEDGMENTS:
The fingerplays, poems, and songs used in FELT BOARD FINGERPLAYS have either been written by the authors or have come from their collection of early childhood education materials. A diligent effort has been made to trace the ownership of all material included. If any errors have occurred, they will be corrected in future editions upon notification of the publishers.

ART:

Cover and Text Illustrations ....Janet McDonnell
                                                        Arlington Heights, Illinois

Cover Design and Layout:................................David Van Delinder
                                                        Studio IVV
                                                        Elgin, Illinois

Text and Graphics Layout: ....Karen Wollscheid
                                                        McHenry, Illinois

PUBLISHED BY:

38W567 Brindlewood
Elgin, Illinois 60123

DISTRIBUTED BY:

Gryphon House
P.O. Box 207
Beltsville, MD 20704

Consortium Book Sales
1045 Westgate Drive
St. Paul, MN 55114

Monarch Books
5000 Dufferin St., Unit K
Downsview, Ontario
Canada M3H 5T5

(Educational Stores & Catalogs)

(U.S. Book Trade)

(All Canadian Orders)

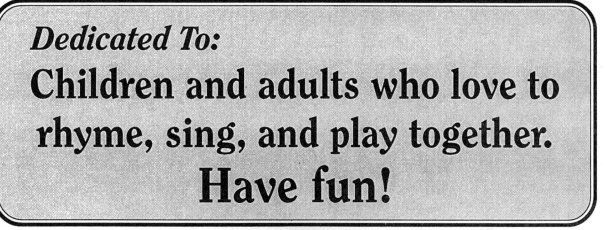

Dedicated To:

Children and adults who love to rhyme, sing, and play together. Have fun!

Contents

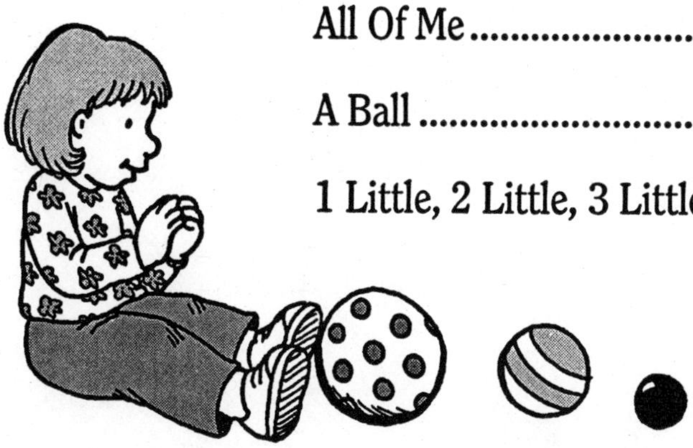

Fall Fingerplays

Hello New Friends

Hello new friends
How are you?
Say your name
And we'll clap for you!
(Let each child say his/her name. Clap for each.)

Eric!

Props

Photograph of each child backed with felt. *(Add a circle of masking tape to the back of each photo if they are too heavy for the felt board.)*

Activity

Have all the photographs upside down on the floor in front of you.

Say HELLO NEW FRIENDS with the children. After you say, *"Say your name,"* slowly put three or four photographs on the felt board. Have each child call out his/her name as you do. Then say the last line and clap for those children. Say the chant again and repeat the activity with three or four more photos. Continue playing until all the photos are on the felt board.

Variation

Dress Yourself – Cut out various skin tone colored construction paper characters. Set them, your collage box, markers, and crayons on the art table. Have the full length mirror at one end of the table. Let each child pick a character and dress him/her. Back each "child" with felt. Write each child's name across his shirt area.

Play HELLO NEW FRIENDS using the characters instead of the photos.

Hello New Friends

Rake The Leaves

Leaves, leaves
   (Arms wave.)
Big and small
   *(Hands and arms far
   apart – Hands close.)*
See if we can rake them all.
   (Raking motion.)

Make

Lots of big and small different colored felt leaves

Props

Basket for the leaves

Activity

Put lots of leaves on the felt board. Have the basket on the floor near the board.

Say to the children, *"I need help raking all these leaves into the basket. Let's say the RAKE THE LEAVES fingerplay."* Say it together and then name two or three children, to come and each "rake-off" a leaf. Before putting it in the basket have each child hold up his leaf and everyone call out "big" or "small" and the leaf's color. For example, *"big red leaf."* Say the rhyme again, and have several more children "rake-off" leaves. Continue until you've "raked" all your leaves into the basket.

Variation

More Difficult – Play the game with small, medium, and large leaves.

Rake The Leaves

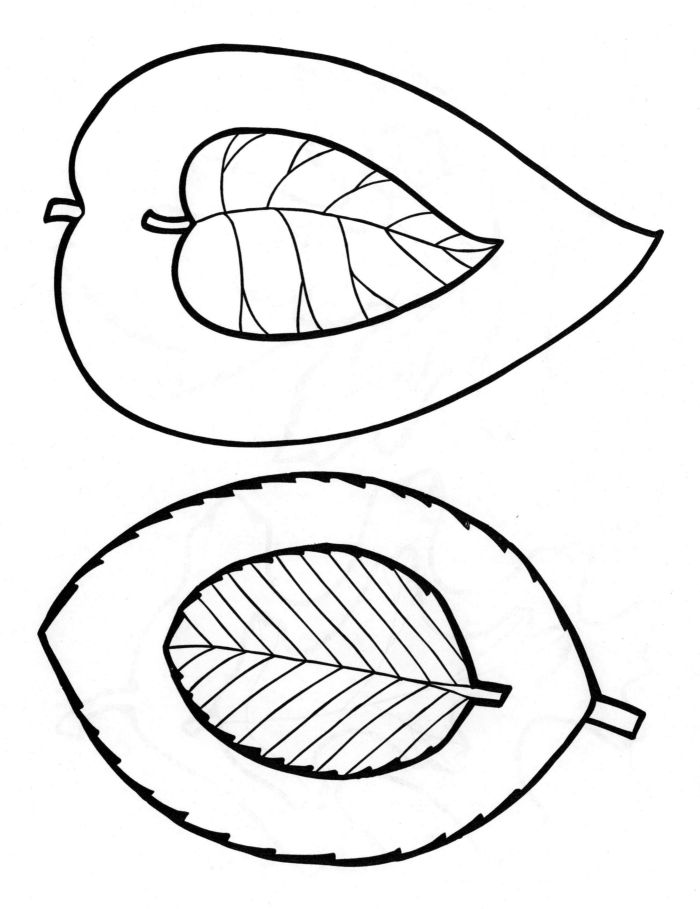

Rake The Leaves

Rake The Leaves

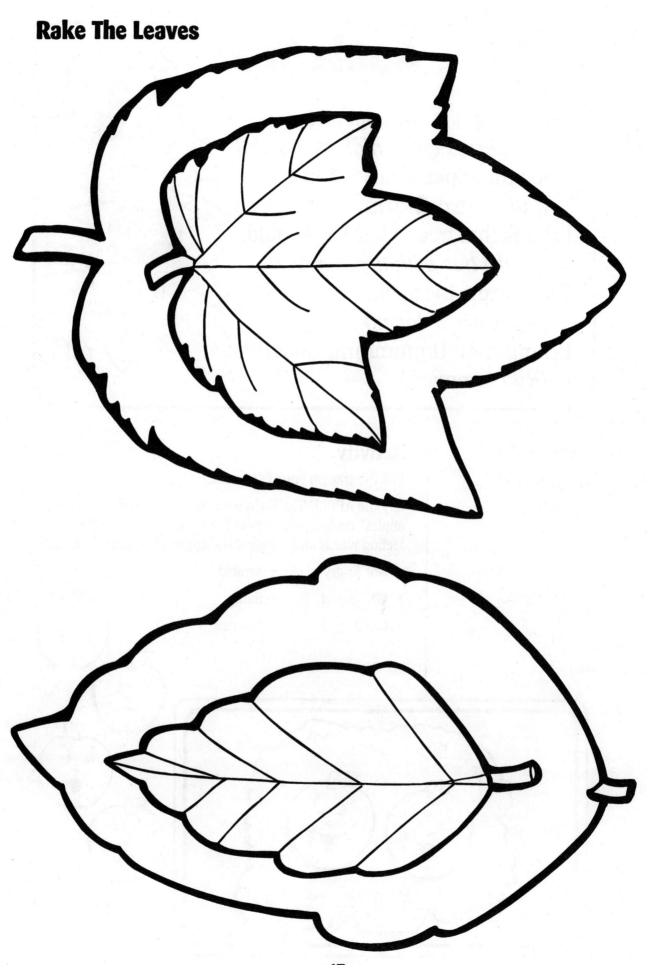

Apple Tree

Way up high in the apple tree.
(Two arms reach high in the air.)
Two little apples smiled at me.
(Put up two fingers.)
I shook that tree as hard as I could.
(Shake tree with two hands.)
Down came the apples.
(Move arms down.)
Ummmmm! Ummmmm! Good!
(Rub tummies.)

Make

Large tree

2 of each apple

Activity

Put the tree on your felt board.

Say the APPLE TREE rhyme and put the pair of "smiling apples" on the tree. Repeat the rhyme using the different feeling words and hanging the appropriate pairs of apples.

- Got Angry
- Smiled
- Whispered
- Sang
- Cried
- Yawned

Apple Tree

Apple Tree

Apple Tree

Name Song

(tune: Farmer In the Dell)

Greg begins with 'G'
Greg begins with 'G'
One clap for Greg, *(Clap for Greg.)*
Greg begins with 'G.'

by Liz Wilmes

Make

Beginning letter alphabet card for each child in your group – remember duplicates.

Activity

Lay all the alphabet cards on the floor in the middle of the group. Let each child find his. *(If they do not recognize their letters, pass them out.)*

Point to one child. Have her hold up her alphabet card. Sing the NAME SONG using her name and first letter. Quietly clap for her as you sing, and then have her put her letter on the felt board.

End the game by singing the ABC SONG.

Name Song

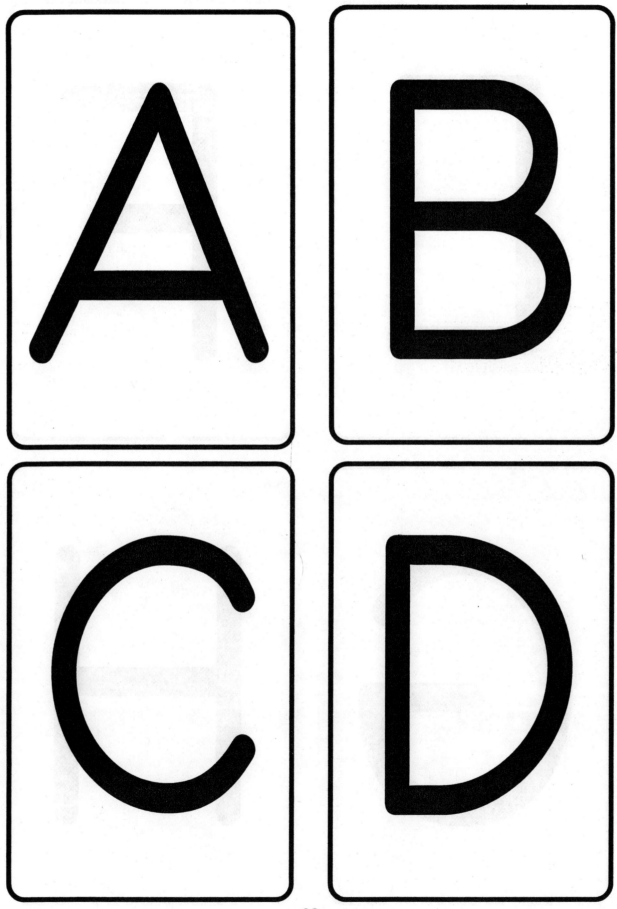

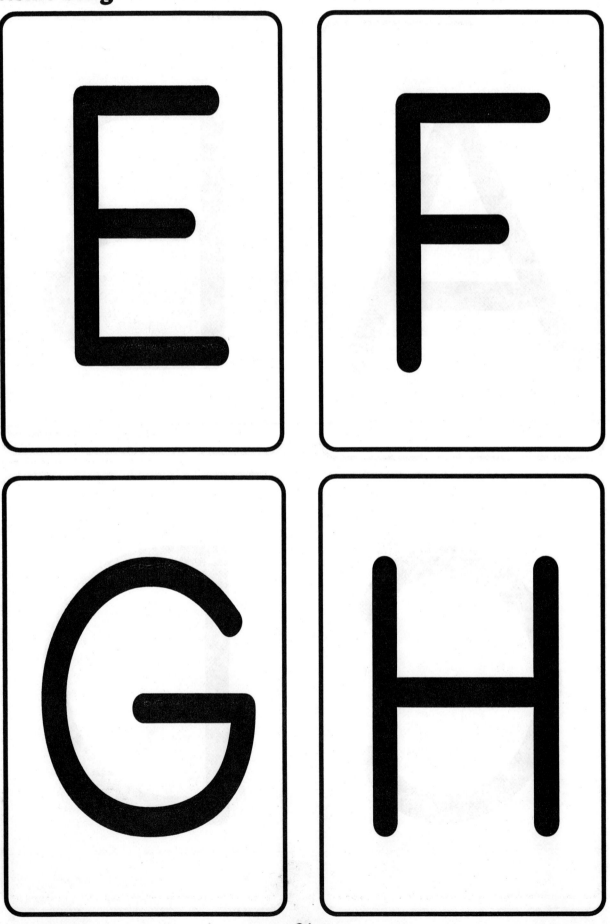

Name Song

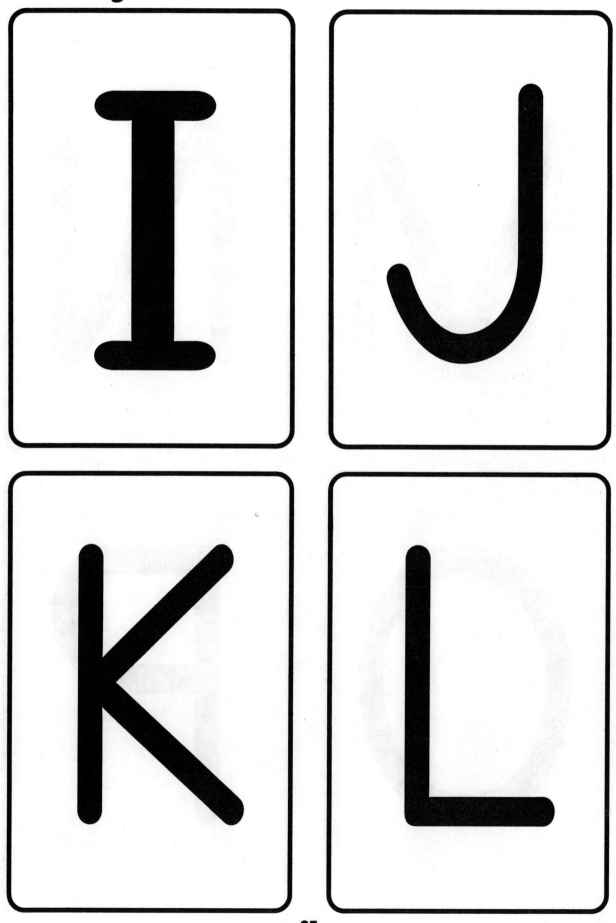

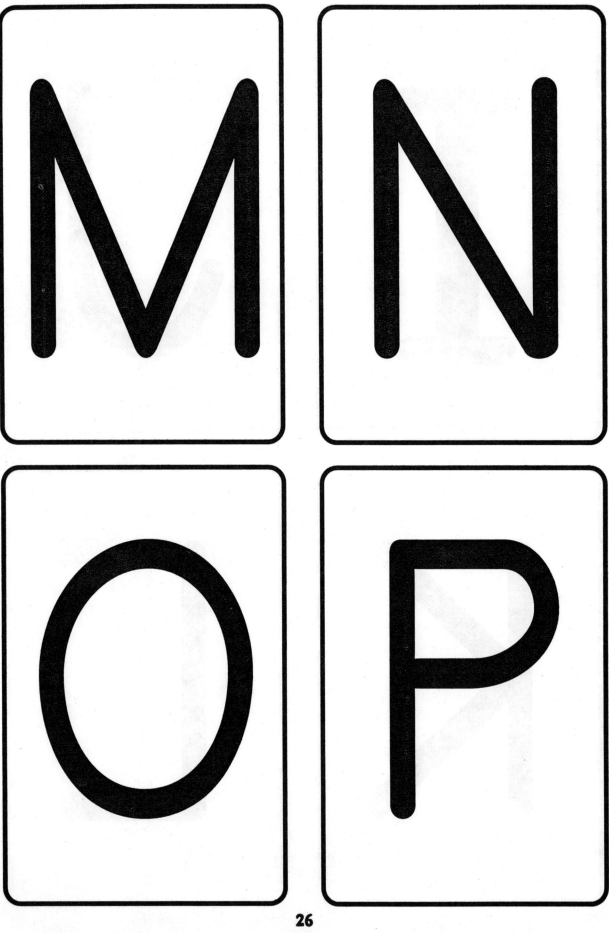

Name Song

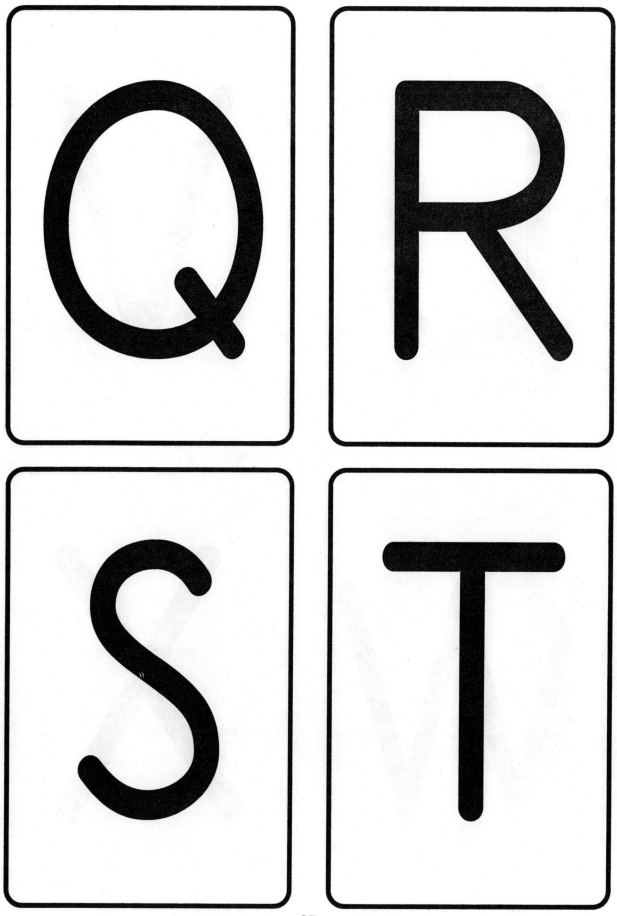

Name Song

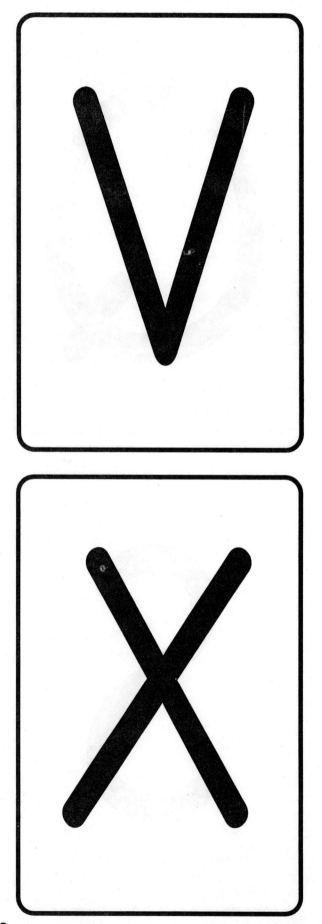

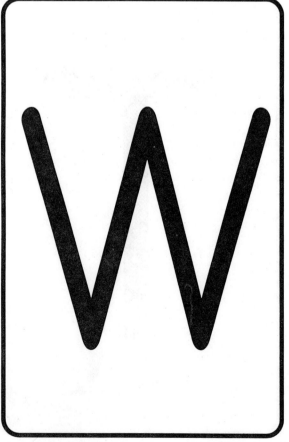

Name Song

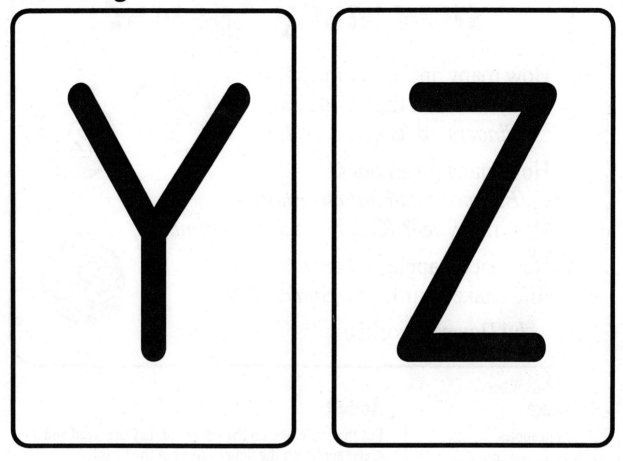

How Many Apples?

How many apples do you see?
Can you count them? 1, 2, 3.
  (Fingers up as you count.)

How many green ones?
  (Everyone call out a number.)
How many red? *(Call out another number.)*

Now eat an apple. *(Chew.)*
And shake your head. *(Shake heads.)*

  by Dawn Zavodsky

Make

3 red apples

3 green apples

Tree

Activity

Put the apple tree on the felt board. Lay the 3 red and 3 green apples on the floor in front of the board.

Have three children come up and each put an apple on the tree. Everyone say HOW MANY APPLES. Point to the apples as you count *"1, 2, 3."* Stop and count the green and red apples as you say the second verse.

Take the apples off the tree. Have three other children come up and each put an apple on the board. Play again.

Variation

More Difficult – Change the fingerplay to different numbers of apples. You could also add yellow apples so you have three kinds to choose from.

How Many Apples?

Let's Build a Scarecrow

First the body, *(Stand up straight.)*
Then the head, *(Touch head.)*
A big straw hat, *(Put on hat.)*
And a scarf of red. *(Put on scarf.)*
Buttons for eyes, *(Touch eyes.)*
A carrot nose, *(Touch nose.)*
A mouth made of stitches,
    (Touch mouth.)
In two smiling rows.
    (Smile at each other.)

Make

Scarecrow shirt

Scarecrow pants

Scarecrow head

Straw hat

Red scarf

2 buttons

Carrot nose

Stitched mouth

Activity

Put the scarecrow shirt and pants on the felt board. Have the other pieces in order in front of you.

Slowly say LET'S BUILD A SCARECROW. As you do, continue to "build the scarecrow."

Let's Build A Scarecrow

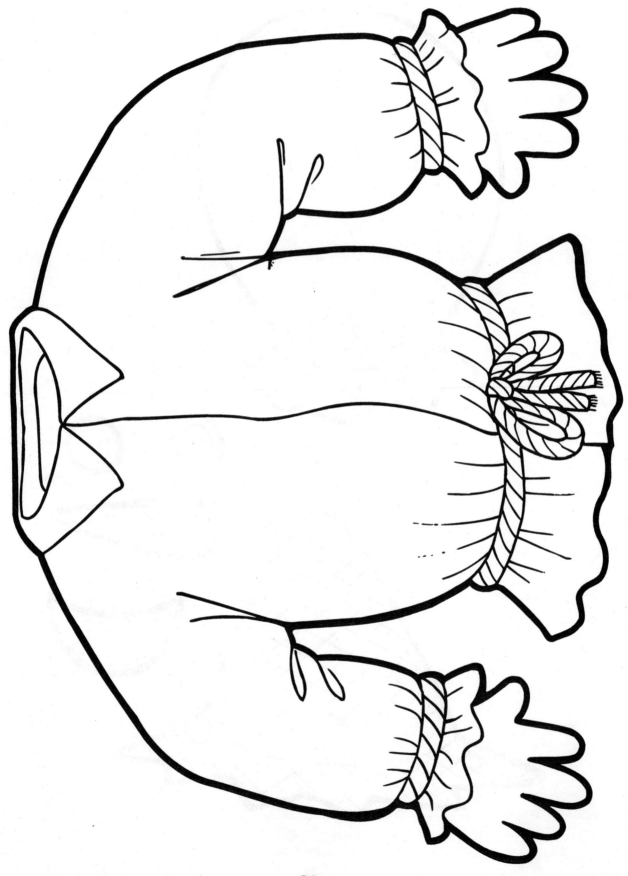

Let's Build A Scarecrow

In The Farmyard

In the farmyard at the end
    of the day,
All the animals politely say,
"Thank you for my food
    today."
The cow says, "Moo."
The pigeon, "Coo."
The sheep says, "Baa."
The lamb says, "Maaa."
The hen, "Cluck, cluck,
    cluck."

"Quack," says the duck.
The dog, "Bow-wow."
The cat, "Meow."
The horse, "Neigh."
The pig grunts, "Oink."
Then the barn is locked up
    tight.
And the farmer quietly says,
    "Good night."

Make

Farmer

Barn

Cow

Pigeon

Sheep

Lamb

Hen

Duck

Dog

Cat

Horse

Pig

(See pages 56-57 for
baby farm animal
patterns.)

Activity

Put the barn on the felt board. Put the animals in front of
you on the floor.

As the group starts to say each line of the rhyme, "walk,
run, gallop," etc. the appropriate animal to the felt board.
Call out the animal and make his "noise." At the end
"walk" the farmer into the farmyard and have him quietly
say *"Good-night"* to all his animals. Then have the
children whisper *"Good-night"* to the farmer.

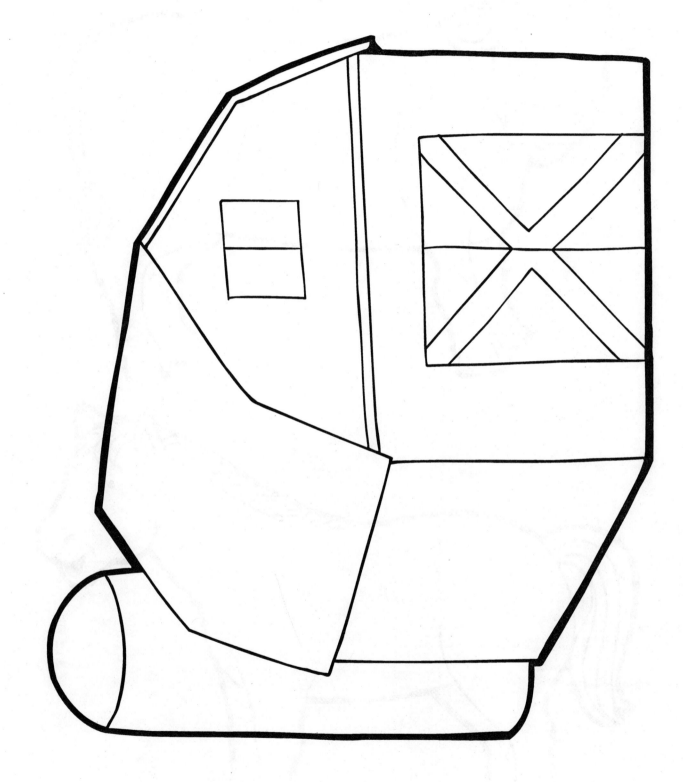

In The Farmyard

In The Farmyard

In The Farmyard

In The Farmyard

Happy Birthday

Happy birthday to you.
   (Point to friends.)
Happy birthday to you.
   (Point to more friends.)
Happy birthday to everyone.
   (Spread out arms.)
Happy birthday to you.
   (Point to friends.)

Make

Birthday cake

At least one candle for each child

Activity

Put the birthday cake on the felt board. Pass out a candle to each child.

Have the children put their candles on the cake. Count as they add each one. Sing HAPPY BIRTHDAY TO EVERYONE. At the end, everyone blow out the candles. Take them down as the children blow.

Variation

Actual Birthdays – Give the birthday child the appropriate number of candles. Let her put them on the cake. Sing HAPPY BIRTHDAY to her. Take the candles down as the children and birthday child blow them out.

Happy Birthday

Stop, Drop, and Roll

Clothes on fire,
Don't get scared.
STOP.
  (Stand still.)
DROP.
  (Lay on floor.)
ROLL.
  (Log roll.)
  by Dick Wilmes

Make

Flame

Child stopping

Child dropping

Child rolling

Activity

Have the four pieces in front of you.

As you say the rhyme, put the pieces on the felt board.

Want More?

Poster – Duplicate the STOP, DROP, AND ROLL Poster. Back it with a piece of colored paper and laminate or cover it with clear adhesive paper. Hang it at the children's eye level.

Stop, Drop, and Roll – Make a posterboard flame. Put a circle of tape on the backside. Have the children sit in a group with a wide open space in the middle.

Ask one child to go into the middle. Give her the flame and have her stick it on herself. Everyone say the STOP, DROP, and ROLL rhyme while the child does the activity. After she's "put out the flame" have her give it to another child and play again.

Stop, Drop and Roll

Clothes on fire,
Don't get scared.

STOP.

DROP.

ROLL.

by Dick Wilmes

Stop, Drop and Roll

Stop, Drop and Roll

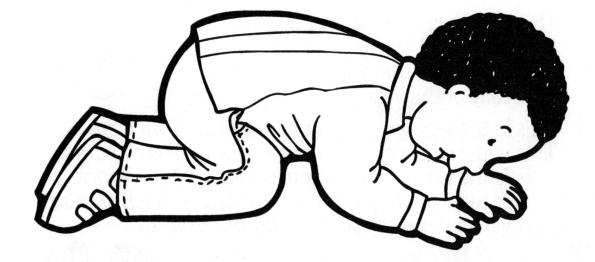

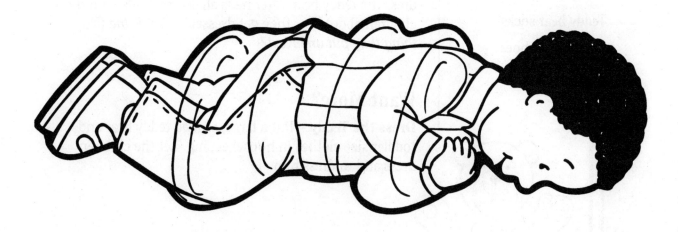

We Get Dressed

(tune: Here We Go Round the Mulberry Bush)

This is the way that we get dressed
We get dressed, we get dressed.
This is the way that we get dressed
Everyday of the year.

This is the way we put on our shirts... *(Touch shirts.)*
This is the way we put on our pants... *(Touch pants.)*
This is the way we put on our socks... *(Touch socks.)*
This is the way we put on our shoes... *(Touch shoes.)*
Last verse: Repeat first verse. *(Stand proud.)*

by Liz Wilmes

Make

Teddy bear

Teddy bear shirt

Teddy bear pants

Teddy bear socks

Teddy bear shoes

Activity

Put the teddy bear on your felt board. Have the clothes in order on the floor.

Begin singing WE GET DRESSED. As you sing each verse, dress the teddy bear. After he is all dressed, talk with the children about how they get dressed. *What is the first thing they put on? Next?*

Want More?

Dress the Teddy – Put a large, stuffed teddy bear and toddler size clothes in housekeeping. Let the children dress and undress him.

We Get Dressed

We Get Dressed
(for warm weather)

We Get Dressed
(for cold weather)

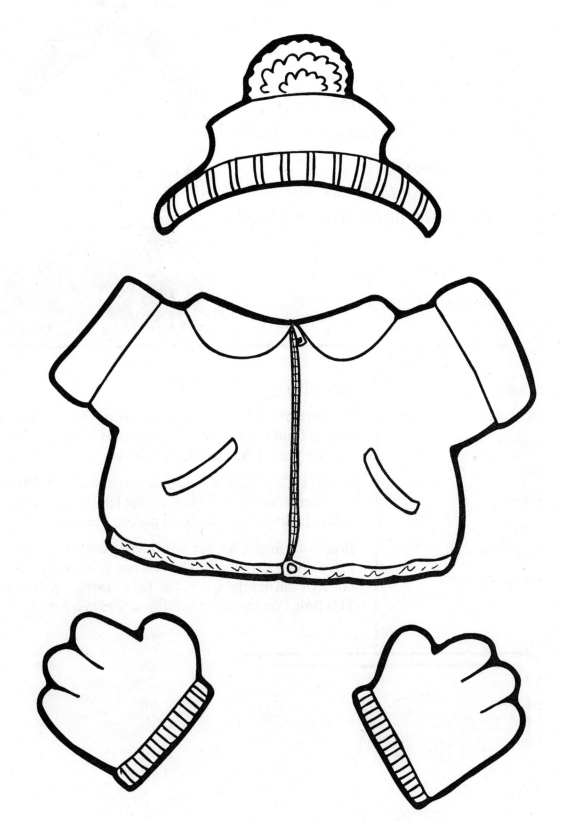

51

What's On a Face?

Here's a face,
Now let's begin.
It has two ears, *(Touch ears.)*
A nose and chin. *(Touch nose/chin.)*

A mouth, two eyes,
    (Touch mouth/eyes.)
With a bushy brow. *(Touch eyebrows.)*
What's on a face?
We all know now!

   by Dick Wilmes

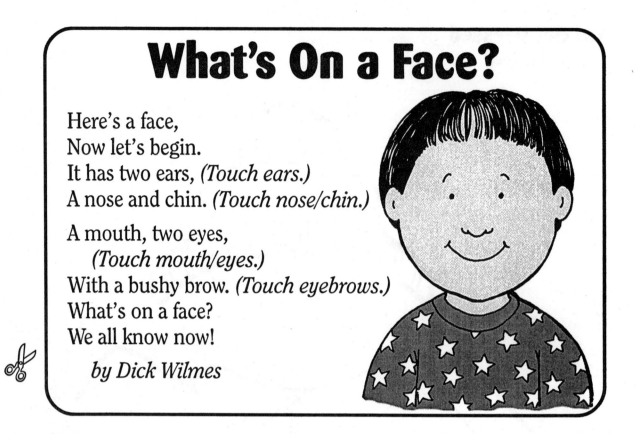

Make

Blank face

Pair of ears

Nose

Chin

Mouth

Pair of eyes

Pair of eyebrows

Activity

Put the blank face on the board. Have all the pieces on the floor in front of you. Place each feature on the face. As you do have the children call out what it is.

Say WHAT'S ON A FACE. As you name each part, have a child come up and point to it on the felt face. Have the other children touch the facial part on themselves.

Repeat the fingerplay, but this time do not say the feature, just point to it on the felt face. As you point, have the children call out the name. Say the fingerplay once more. This time take the feature off the face as everyone says it.

What's On A Face?

Old McDonald

Old McDonald had a farm – E-I-E-I-O
And on his farm he had a cow – E-I-E-I-O
With a "moo-moo" here and a
    "moo-moo" there,
Here a "moo," there a "moo"
Everywhere a "moo-moo."

Continue with other
animals and their sounds.

MOO!

Make

Farmer

Barn

Cow

Goat

Duck

Dog

Cat

Horse

Pig

(See pages 38-41 for adult farm animal patterns.)

Activity

Put Old McDonald and the barn on your felt board. Have all the baby farm animals on the floor in front of you.

As you sing the line, *"And on his farm he had a ..."* point to a child. Have him call out an animal. Put that animal on the board near the barn. Continue singing that verse. Start the next verse. At the appropriate time, point to another child and have her name a second animal. Put that one on the board. Continue until the farmyard is full of Farmer McDonald's animals.

After all the animals are on the board, pretend that it is night time. Very quietly say to the children, *"Time for all the animals to go to sleep. Good night, _____."*
Continue taking them down, whispering, *"Good night"* to each one.

Old McDonald

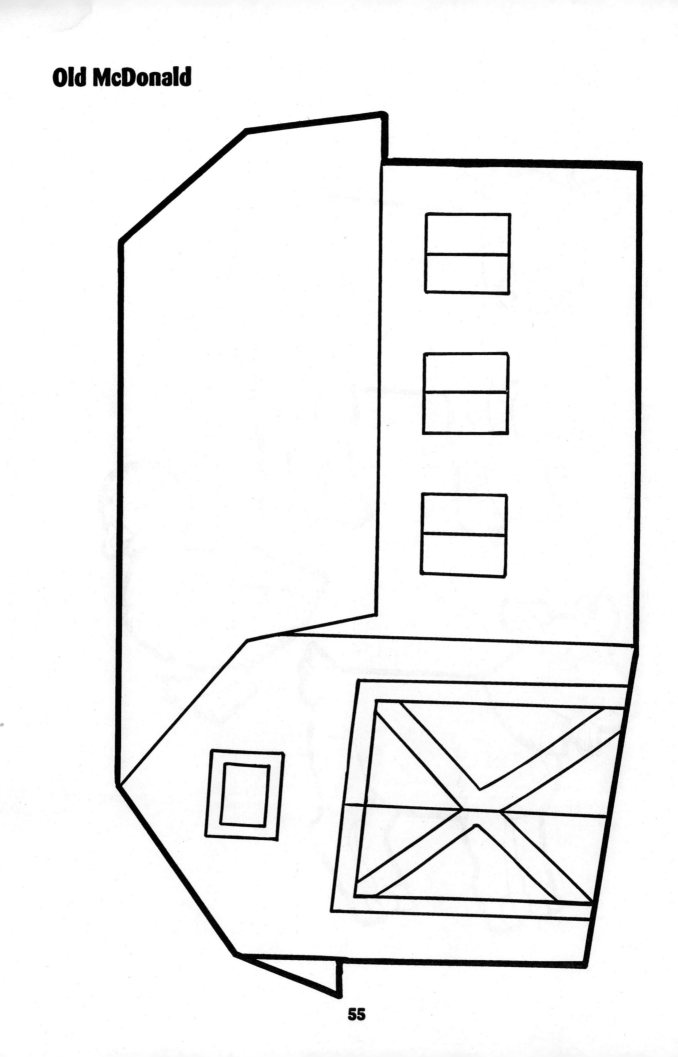

Old McDonald

Old McDonald

This Is Jack-O-Happy

This is Jack-O-Happy. *(Make happy face.)*
This is Jack-O-Sad. *(Make sad face.)*
This is Jack-O-Sleepy. *(Make sleepy face.)*
This is Jack-O-Mad. *(Make mad face.)*
This is Jack-O-Broken *(Hold hands out to
    serve pumpkin pie.)*
Into pieces small
Baked in a pumpkin pie
That's the best of all. *(Rub tummies.)*
YUM! YUM!

Make

Happy jack-o-lantern

Sad jack-o-lantern

Sleepy jack-o-lantern

Mad jack-o-lantern

Pieces of a
jack-o-lantern

Pumpkin pie

Activity

Have the felt pieces in order on the floor in front of you.

Say THIS IS JACK-O-HAPPY with the children. As you say each line, put the appropriate jack-o-lantern on the board. Afterwards, point to the first jack-o-lantern, have the children call out his name, and then take him off the felt board. Repeat for each one.

Start the rhyme again by saying, *"This is _____."* As you're talking, put Jack-O-Happy on the felt board. Have the children finish the line. Continue in the same manner letting the children fill in the jack-o-lantern's name when you pause.

This Is Jack-O-Happy

This Is Jack-O-Happy

This Is Jack-O-Happy

Turkey Feathers

(tune: Are You Sleeping?)

Turkey feathers, turkey feathers
Brightly colored, brightly colored.
Who has a red one?
   Who has a red one?
Add it now. Add it now.

by Liz Wilmes

Make

Large turkey

Lots of different colored feathers.
(At least 2 for each child.)

Activity

Put the turkey on the felt board. Lay all the feathers in a large basket or shallow box, so the children can easily see them.

Walk around the group of children. Let each child pick a turkey feather. Walk around again and let each child choose another one. Continue if there are any left.

Sing TURKEY FEATHERS with the children. Name a color and let the children who have that color add it to the turkey. Sing again, naming another color and adding those feathers to the turkey. Continue until the turkey is showing off all his feathers.

Turkey Feathers

Which One Is Missing?

(tune: Are You Sleeping?)

Turkey feathers, turkey feathers
Red, yellow, green – red, yellow, green.
Which one is missing?
Which one is missing?
Name it now.
Name it now.

by Liz Wilmes

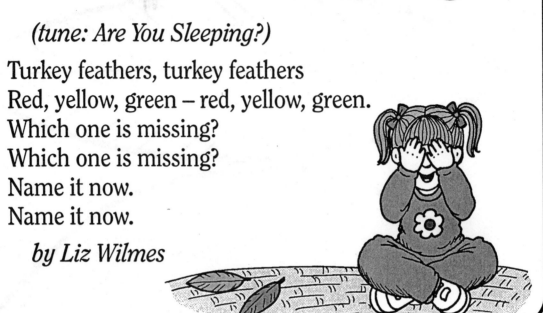

Make

Turkey

2 or more red feathers

2 or more yellow feathers

2 or more green feathers

Activity

Put the turkey on the felt board. In random order, put two or more red, yellow, and green feathers on him.

Have the children cover their eyes. Take two or more feathers off the turkey. Have the children uncover their eyes, and look carefully at the turkey as they sing WHICH ONES ARE MISSING. After they've finished singing, have them call out which feathers they think are missing. As they do, bring that feather back and put it on the turkey. Play again and again, mixing up the colors and numbers of feathers you remove each time.

Which One Is Missing?

Winter Fingerplays

Snow Pants

(tune: Here We Go 'Round the Mulberry Bush)

This is the way we put on snow pants, *(Put on snow pants.)*
Put on snow pants, put on snow pants.
This is the way we put on snow pants,
All on a snowy morning.

This is the way we put on our boots... *(Put on boots.)*
This is the way we put on our coat... *(Put on coat.)*
This is the way we put on our scarf... *(Put on scarf.)*
This is the way we put on our hat... *(Put on hat.)*
This is the way we put on our mittens... *(Put on mittens.)*

Make

Child

Snow pants

Snow boots

Coat

Scarf

Hat

Mittens

Activity

Put the child on the felt board. Have the snow clothes on the floor for everyone to see.

Talk about getting dressed for winter play. As you talk about the different articles of clothing, have the children help you dress the felt child. After he is all dressed, undress him in the order in which children would take off their snow clothes. Have the children call out the names of the clothing as you do.

Now sing SNOW PANTS and dress the felt child. Encourage the children to pretend to put on their snow clothes as they sing.

Snow Pants

Snow Pants

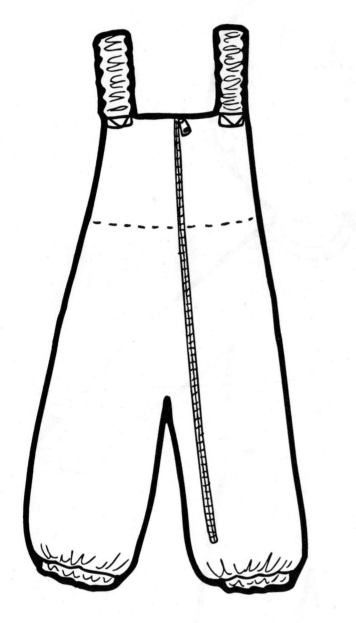

Snow Pants

Snow

Snow on my forehead, *(Touch forehead.)*
Snow on my knee, *(Touch knee.)*
Snow on my glasses, *(Touch eyes.)*
Getting hard to see.

Snow on my boots, *(Touch shoes.)*
Snow on my hair, *(Touch hair.)*
Snow on my mittens, *(Touch hands.)*
Snow everywhere. *(Wave hands all over.)*

by Dick Wilmes

Make

Child dressed for snow play

Lots of snowflakes

Activity

Put the child on the felt board.

Say the fingerplay slowly. As you do, have everyone touch each place on his body where the snow is falling. Talk about playing in the snow.

Pass out several snowflakes to each child. Say the rhyme to them. As you do, have them think about where they want to put their snowflakes. Now say the rhyme together. Stop after each line and let the children who want, put their snowflakes on the child. Continue until the end. If any children still have snowflakes, have them put theirs on the board.

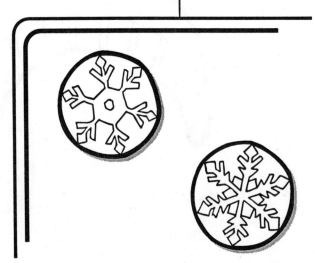

Snow

Pet Voices

(adapted traditional rhyme)

I'm a dog – hear me bark! *(Talk like a dog.)*
I'm a cat – hear me purr! *(Talk like a cat.)*
I'm a mouse – hear me squeak! *(Talk like a mouse.)*
I'm a fish – hear me breath! *(Wiggle lips.)*
I'm a chick – hear me cheep! *(Talk like a chick.)*
I'm a bird – hear me chirp! *(Talk like a bird.)*
I'm really a child – hear me laugh!! *(Laugh.)*

Make

Dog

Cat

Mouse

Fish

Rabbit

Bird

Boy and girl

Activity

Have all the pet pieces in front of you so everyone can see them. Hide the boy and girl behind your back.

Say to the children, *"I'm a* (put the dog on the felt board). Children call out *"dog."* You say, *"Hear me _____."* The children bark like dogs. Continue this "fill in the blank" game as you put the rest of the pets on the felt board.

At the end, bring out the two children and everyone laugh together.

Pet Voices

Pet Voices

Pet Voices

Five Little Snowpals

Five little snowpals standing in a row.
(Dance five fingers.)
Each has a hat and big red bow.
(Put had on head/scarf on neck.)
Out came the sun and it shown all day.
(Arms in circle overhead.)
One little snowpal melted away.
(Wiggle arms to floor.)

Repeat with 4...3...2...1 snowpals.

Make

5 snowpals

Sun

Activity

Lay the sun next to you on the floor. Pass out the five snowpals to five children. Have them put the five snowpals in a row near the top of the felt board.

Say FIVE LITTLE SNOWPALS with the children. As you say the third line, put the sun over one of the snowpals and then have him "melt away" to the bottom of the board. Count the remaining snowpals with the children. Say the fingerplay again. Continue until all five snowpals have melted away.

Five Little Snowpals

Five Little Snowpals

Five Little Snowpals

Dear Old Frosty

(tune: Mary Had a Little Lamb)

Guess who wears a magic hat,
Magic hat, magic hat.
Guess who wears a magic hat,
Dear Old Frosty.

Guess who has two eyes of coal… *(Touch eyes.)*
Guess who has a carrot nose…*(Touch nose.)*
Guess who carries a big yellow broom…*(Sweep.)*
Guess who wears a big red scarf…*(Tie scarf.)*
Guess who wears big green mittens…*(Hold up hands.)*
Guess who wears big black boots…*(March feet.)*

by Liz Wilmes

Make

Frosty

Magic hat

Coal eyes

Carrot nose

Broom

Scarf

Mittens

Big boots

Props

Several magic hats

Activity

Put Frosty on the felt board. Have the rest of the pieces in the order you will need them. Stack them in a pile and put them nearby.

Sing DEAR OLD FROSTY with the children. As you sing, dress him.

Want More?

Dance Like Frosty – Put on some peppy dance music. Give 3-4 children "magic hats" and let them dance in the middle. Stop the music, have the children quickly give their hats to others. Start the music and let the Frosties dance some more.

Dear Old Frosty

Dear Old Frosty

Dear Old Frosty

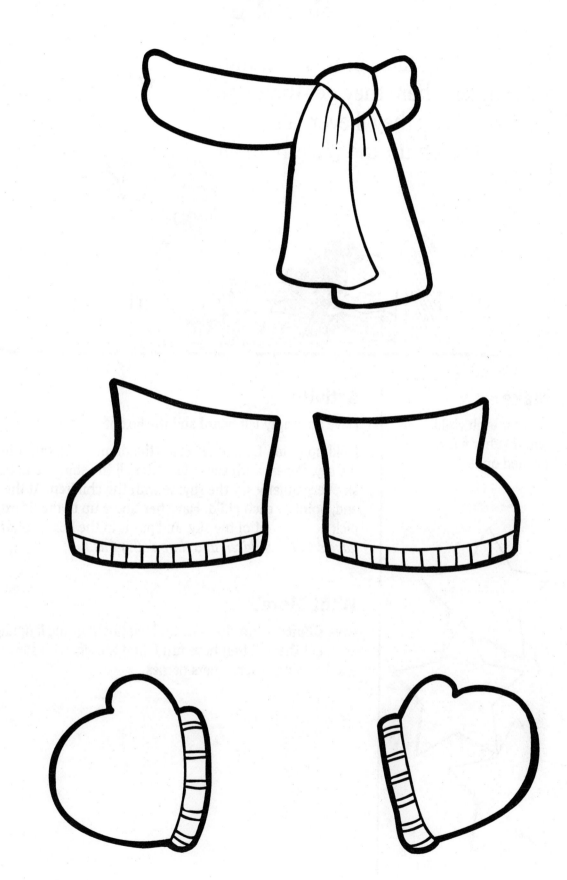

Stars

I watch the stars come out at night.
I wonder where they get their light.
I don't think they'll ever fall.
So, I'll reach up and pick them all.

Make

Star for each child with his/her name printed on it

Activity

Have an empty felt board and the box of felt stars.

Hold up a star. Everyone "read" the name on it. Put it in the sky. Repeat with each star. After all the stars are in the sky, very quietly say the rhyme with the children. At the end, point to each child. Have her tiptoe up to the board, pick her star out of the sky, and put it in the box. *(Could have several children at a time doing this.)*

Want More?

Free Choice – Put the stars and felt board in the language area. Let the children have fun filling the sky with stars and "reading" each others names.

Stars

Buying a Donut

Down around the corner
In the bakery shop,
There were lots of little donuts
With frosting on top.
Along came *(child's name)* all alone.
She bought a *(color)* one and
    ran on home.

Make

Different colored doughnuts *(several more than the number of children you have)*

Activity

Lay the felt board in the middle of the group of children. Pretend it is a bakery box. Lay all the donuts in the "box."

Name a child. Have her skip, walk, etc. around the area and think about her favorite donut as everyone says BUYING A DONUT. At the last verse, say the child's name and the color donut she "bought."

Repeat until all the children have donuts. Go on a pretend snack. *"How were your donuts?"*

Buying a Donut

Head, Shoulders, Knees, and Toes

Head, shoulders, knees, and toes,
   (Touch body parts as you sing.)
Knees and toes, knees and toes.
Head, shoulders, knees, and toes.
Eyes, ears, mouth, and nose.

Make

Small or large child

Activity

Put the child on the felt board.

Point to the felt child's body parts as you sing HEAD, SHOULDERS, KNEES, AND TOES. Let the children touch their real parts.

Sing again, only this time, when you get to the fourth line, let four children name other body parts. As each child names a part, you point to it on the felt child and all the children will point to their real part.

Head, Shoulders, Knees, Toes

Head, Shoulders, Knees, Toes

I Can Even Count Some More

One, two, three, four,
(Hold up four fingers.)
I can even count some more.
Five, six, seven, eight,
(Hold up fingers on other hand.)
Nine, ten are my thumb men.
(Hold up two thumbs.)

Make

10 number cards

Activity

Have the number cards in order in front of you.

Slowly say I CAN EVEN COUNT SOME MORE. As you say it, put the number cards in order on the felt board. Now say the fingerplay at a regular pace, pointing to each number as you go. Now say it fast, taking the numbers off the felt board.

I Can Even Count Some More

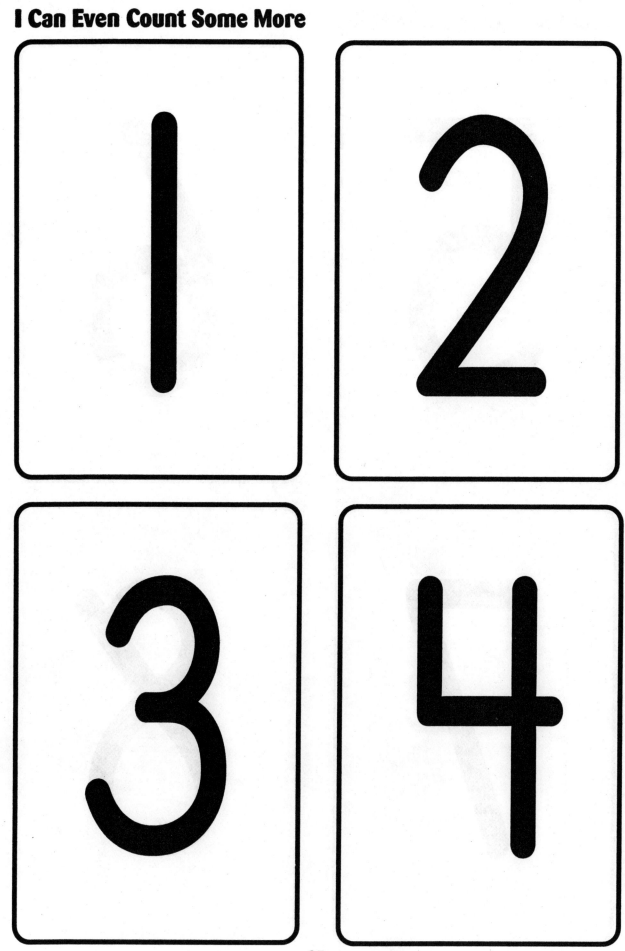

I Can Even Count Some More

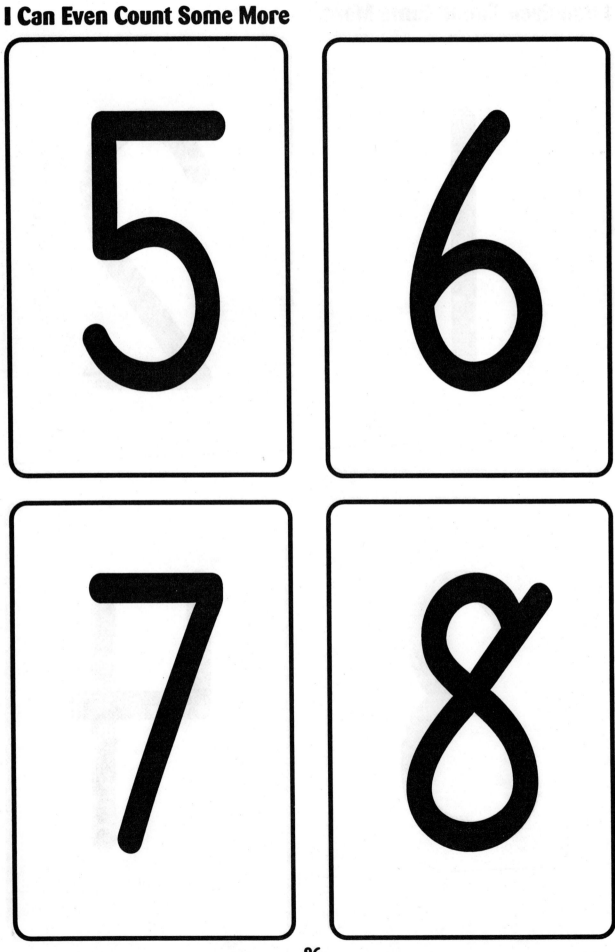

5

6

7

8

I Can Even Count Some More

Here Are My Ears

Here are my ears.
  (Touch body parts.)

Here is my nose.

Here are my fingers.

Here are my toes.

Here are my eyes,

Both open wide.

Here is my mouth,

With white teeth inside.

Here is my tongue,

That helps me speak.

Here is my chin.

Here are my cheeks.

Here are my hands,

That help me play.

Here are my feet,

For walking today.

Make

Large child *(See pages 92-93 for pattern.)*

Activity

Put the child on the felt board.

You say the rhyme to the children. Instead of saying the body part in each line, point to it on the felt board child and have the children name it.

Want More?

Here Is – Say *"Here is my ..."* As you talk, point to a body part on the felt child that was not in the fingerplay. Have the children call it out. Keep repeating the opening line, *"Here is my..."* and pointing to another part.

Winter Walk – After saying the rhyme, put on your winter clothes and take a walk around the neighborhood.

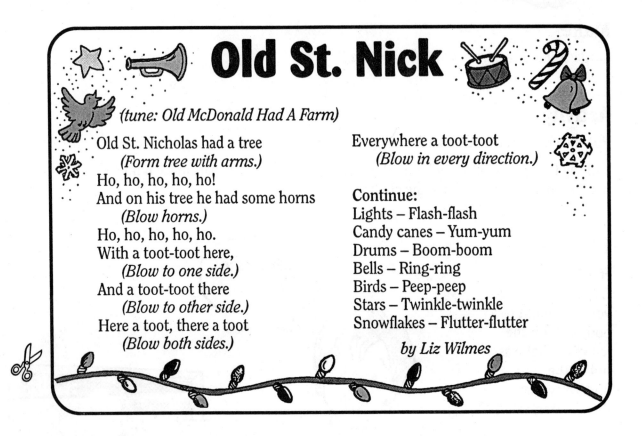

Old St. Nick

(tune: Old McDonald Had A Farm)

Old St. Nicholas had a tree
   (Form tree with arms.)
Ho, ho, ho, ho, ho!
And on his tree he had some horns
   (Blow horns.)
Ho, ho, ho, ho, ho.
With a toot-toot here,
   (Blow to one side.)
And a toot-toot there
   (Blow to other side.)
Here a toot, there a toot
   (Blow both sides.)

Everywhere a toot-toot
   (Blow in every direction.)

Continue:
Lights – Flash-flash
Candy canes – Yum-yum
Drums – Boom-boom
Bells – Ring-ring
Birds – Peep-peep
Stars – Twinkle-twinkle
Snowflakes – Flutter-flutter

by Liz Wilmes

Make

Evergreen tree

Horn/s

Light/s

Candy cane/s

Drum/s

Bell/s

Bird/s

Snowflake/s

Star/s

Activity

Put the evergreen tree on the felt board. Lay the ornaments in a box so the children can easily see them.

Hold up and name each type of ornament so the children can see what is in the box. Walk around the group and let each child choose an ornament. Walk again and let them choose again.

Sing the first verse of OLD ST. NICK. Let the children who have horns, put them on the tree. Continue singing and decorating the tree until all the ornaments are displayed.

Old St. Nick

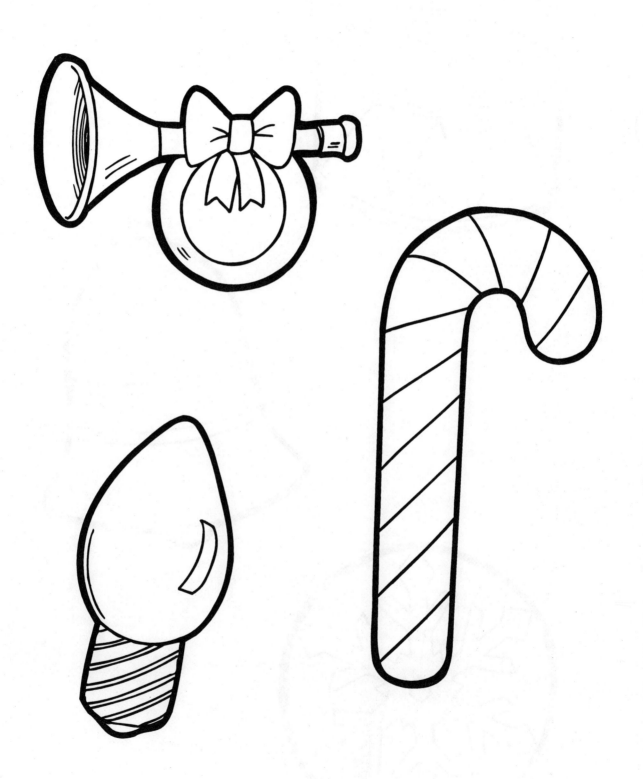

Old St. Nick

Old St. Nick

Old St. Nick

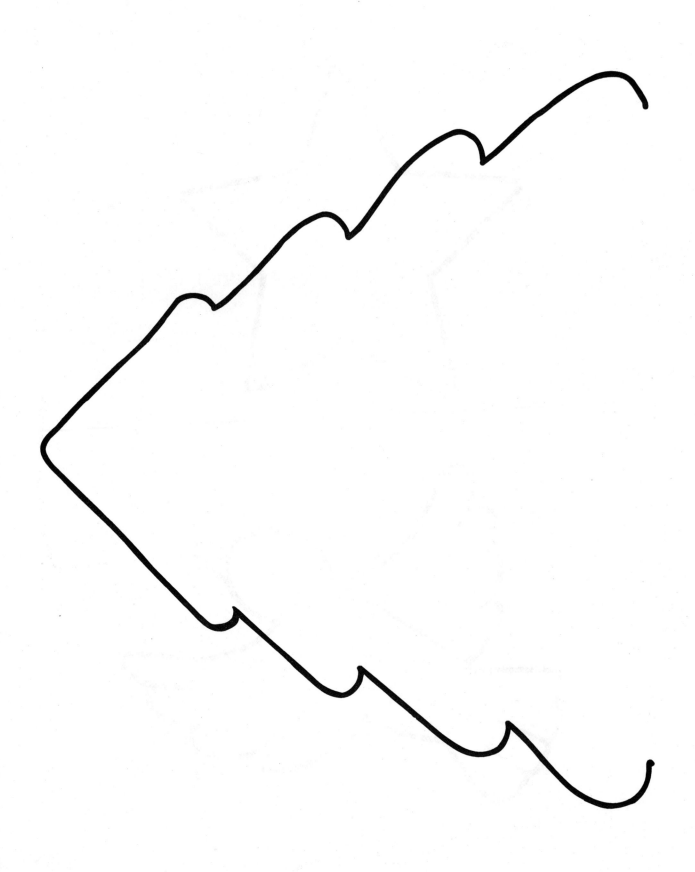

Old St. Nick

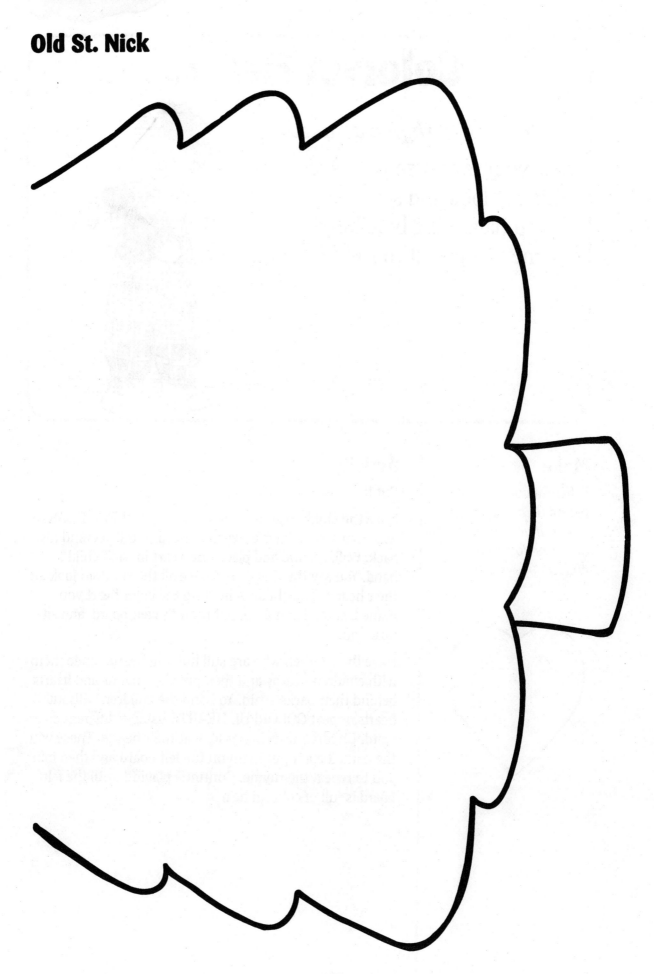

Colorful Hearts

(traditional rhyme adapted)

Use your eyes, use your eyes,
You can look and see.
If you have a big blue heart,
Come and give it to me.

Make

Different colored large hearts *(Duplicates are fine, but you need at least one for each child.)*

Activity

Put the hearts in a pile.

Have the children sit in a circle. Say COLORFUL HEARTS with them. Now have everyone put his hands behind his back. Walk around and place one heart in each child's hand. You say the rhyme and have all the children look at their hearts. The children holding the color heart you named, should come up, put it on the felt board, and sit near you.

Have the children who are still holding hearts, trade them with children nearby and then put their hands and hearts behind their backs again. You and the children without hearts, repeat COLORFUL HEARTS using a different color word. Children with hearts look at their hearts. Those with the named color put them on the felt board and then join you to repeat the rhyme. Continue playing until the felt board is full of colorful hearts

Colorful Hearts

1 Little, 2 Little, 3 Little Hearts

(tune: 1 Little, 2 Little, 3 Little Children)

1 little, 2 little, 3 little hearts,
   (Put fingers up as you sing.)
4 little, 5 little, 6 little hearts,
7 little, 8 little, 9 little hearts,
Bring love on Valentines Day

Make

9 graduated hearts with numerals 1-9 on them

Activity

Put the hearts in order in front of you on the floor.

Teach the children 1 LITTLE, 2 LITTLE, 3 LITTLE HEARTS. Sing it again, putting the felt hearts on the board as you sing each number. Now sing the song backwards, taking the hearts off the felt board as you sing the numbers.

Want More?

Put the Hearts In Order – Put the felt board and the hearts on the discovery table. Encourage the children to put them in order from largest to smallest and smallest to largest. Read the numerals on the hearts.

1 Little, 2 Little, 3 Little Hearts

Spring Fingerplays

Ant Hill

Once I saw an ant hill, *(Make fist.)*
With no ants about.
So I asked, "Dear little ants, *(Talk to "ants" in fist.)*
Won't you please come out?"

Then, as if the little ants
Had heard my call.
One, two, three, four, five came out!
    (Hold up fingers.)
Marching very tall. *(March hand.)*

Make

12" diameter felt circle for the "ant hill"

5 marching ants

Activity

Put the five ants close together in the middle of the felt board. Cover them with the "ant hill."

Say the fingerplay with the children as if you are talking to the "ant hill" on your felt board. Slowly count *"1, 2, 3, 4, 5"* as the ants come "marching" out from their hill.

Want More?

Which Ant Is Largest – Put all the ants in mixed up order on the felt board. Let the child put them in order from largest to smallest – smallest to largest

Ant Hill

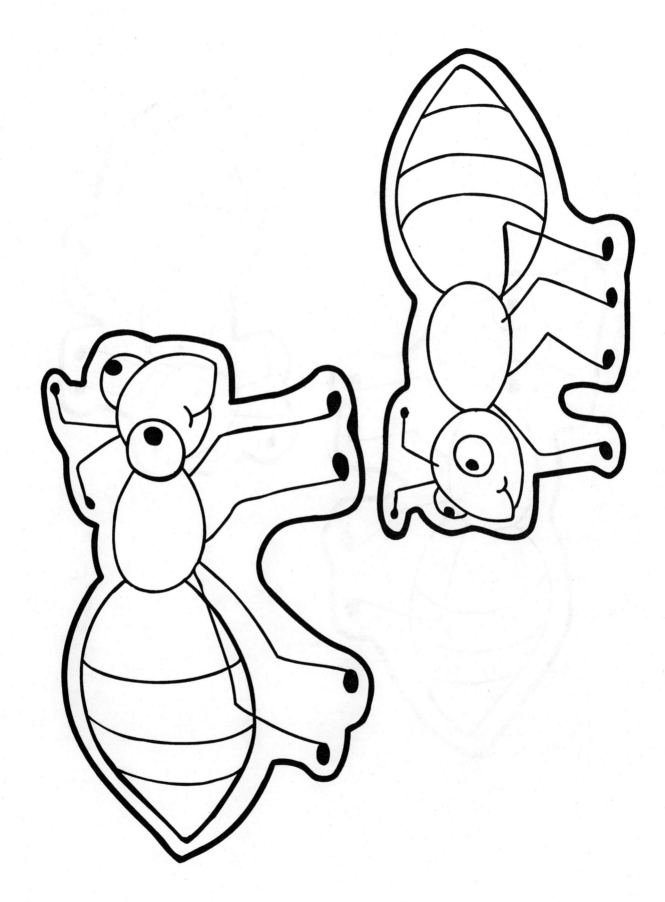

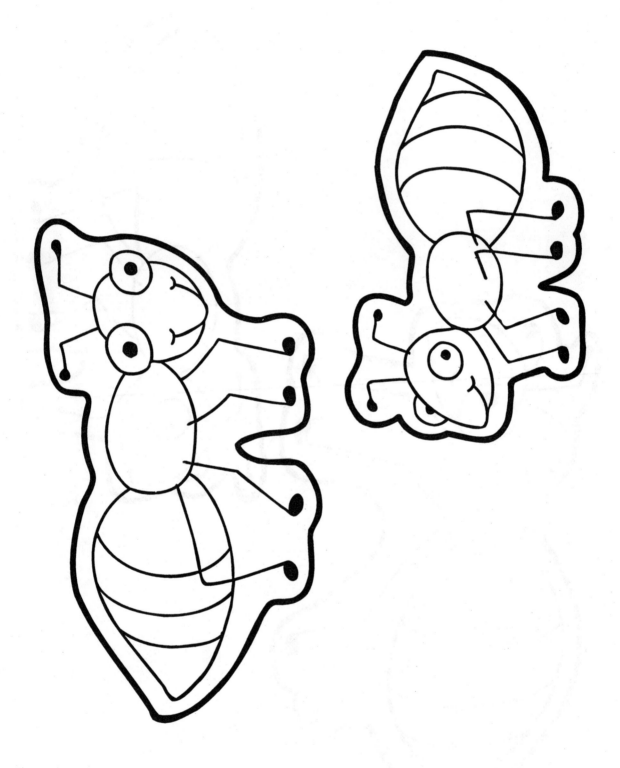

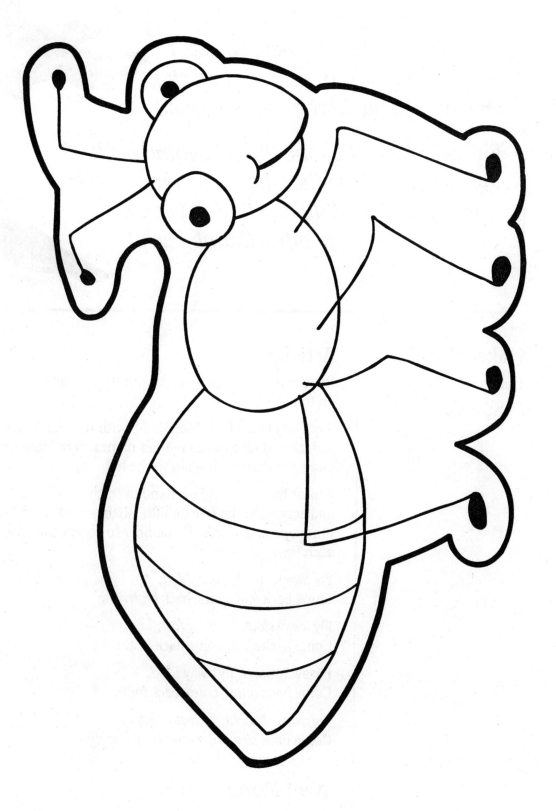

Two Little Blackbirds

Two little blackbirds
Sitting on the hill. *(Make two fists.)*
One named Jack, *(Raise one thumb.)*
One named Jill. *(Raise other thumb.)*

Fly away Jack. *(Fly one thumb behind back.)*
Fly away Jill. *(Fly other thumb behind back.)*
Come back Jack. *(Fly one thumb back.)*
Come back Jill. *(Fly other thumb back.)*

Make

Hill
2 blackbirds

Activity

Put the hill on the felt board with the two blackbirds on top.

Say TWO LITTLE BLACKBIRDS with the children. Point to Jack and Jill as you say their names. "Fly" each one away and then back again to the hill.

Repeat the fingerplay over and over, changing the words and actions in the fourth, fifth, sixth, and seventh lines to other opposite words. Remember to accent the opposites each time.

Fly away *low*, fly away *high*.
Come back *low*, come back *high*.

Fly away *slow*, fly away *fast*.
Come back *slow*, come back fast.

Fly away *quiet*, fly away *loud*.
Come back *quiet*, come back *loud*.

Fly away *straight*, fly away *wiggly*.
Come back *straight*, come back *wiggly*.

Want More?

Two Little Redbirds – Use a different pair of colored birds each time you say the fingerplay.

Two Little Blackbirds

Bug In the Rug

Bug in the rug,
Bug in the rug,
Who is that
Bug in the rug?

Make

Rug

Beetle

Ladybug

Ant

Spider

Mosquito

Fly

Bee

Activity

Put the bugs in the middle of the felt board. Put the rug off to one side, near the top of the felt board.

Have the children cover their eyes and say the rhyme. While they are saying it, put one or two bugs under the rug. At the end of the rhyme, have the children open their eyes and call out what bug/s they think are hiding under the rug. Lift the rug and name the bug/s.

Play again and again. To make it more difficult, mix up the order of the bugs every couple of times.

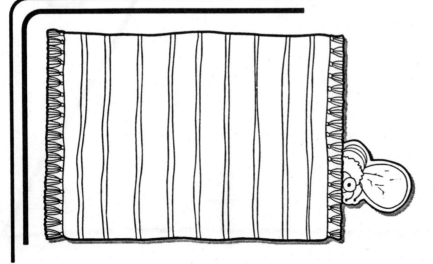

Bug in the Rug

Bug in the Rug

Bug in the Rug

Bees Everywhere

Bees here,
　　(Flash hands to the left.)
Bees there,
　　(Flash hands to the right.)
Bees, bees
Everywhere!
　　(Spread hands.)

Make

Bees for all the children *(Several different colors and expressions.)*

Bear

Hive

Activity

Put the bear in the middle of the felt board. Pass out at least one bee to each child. Place the hive behind the board.

Have each child put his bee on the felt board. As he does say, *"(Child's name) is putting his bee under the bear's foot."* or *"(Child's name) is putting her bee far away from the bear."* Continue until all the bees are on, around, and under the big bear.

Say BEES EVERYWHERE with the children.

Now put the hive in a corner of the board. Say to the children, *"The bees have been playing with the bear for a long time. They are really tired and want to fly back to their hive. They will need your help."* Tell each child which bee to fly back to the hive. For example, *"(Child's name) fly the bee that is between the bear's eyes back to the hive."* Continue until all the bees are in the hive. *"Good-night, bees."*

Bees Everywhere

123

Bees Everywhere

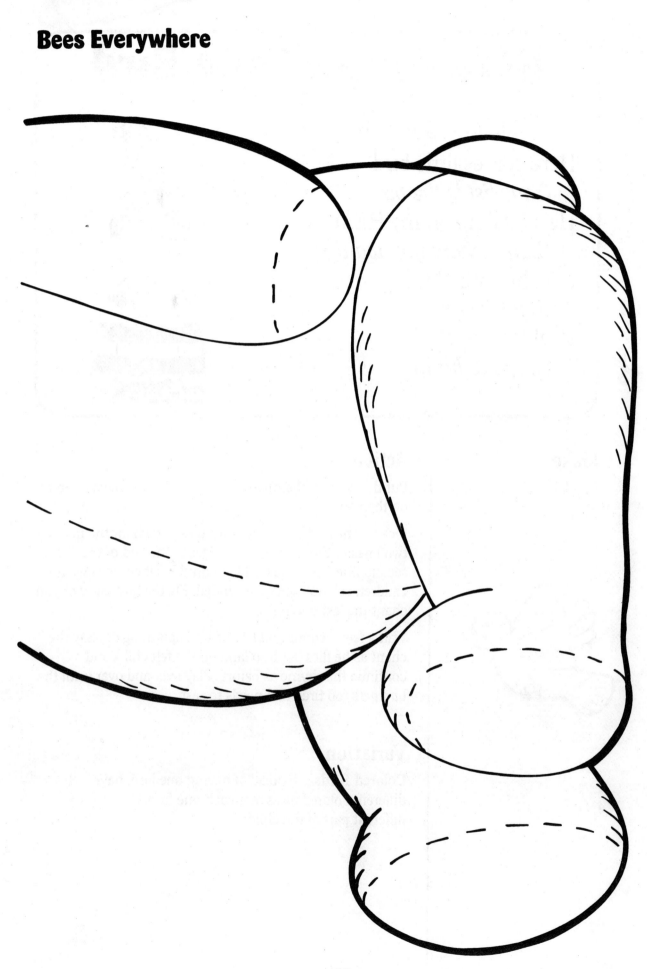

Here Comes Little Bird

(Chant or say this rhyme.)

Here comes little bird.
(Your fist is the bird.)
He's landing on my HEAD.
(Land where you want.)
Bye, bye little bird.
(Fly bird away.)
Bye! Bye! Bye!
(Wave to bird.)

Make

Child

Bird

Activity

Put the child in the middle of the felt board. Have the bird on the floor.

Pick up the bird and fly it around as you chant the first two lines of the rhyme. As you get to the end of the second line, have the bird land on the felt child. Have the children call out where he landed. Fly the bird away as you chant the last two lines.

Wait a few seconds and let the bird appear again. Say the chant as he flies, let him land on the felt child, and continue the rhyme as before. Play over and over until the bird gets too tired and needs to rest.

Variation

Colored Birds – Instead of having one bird, have 7-8 different colored birds. Let each one fly and land on a different part of the child.

Here Comes Little Bird

H-I-P-P-O

(tune: BINGO)

There was a girl/boy who had a pet
And HIPPO was his name, oh!
H-I-P-P-O, H-I-P-P-O, H-I-P-P-O
And HIPPO was his name, oh!

by Liz Wilmes

Repeat with other zoo animals – Panda, Rhino,
Whale, Tiger, Camel, Snake, Zebra

Make

Zoo animals with
nameplates

- Hippopotamus
- Panda
- Rhinoceros
- Whale
- Camel
- Tiger
- Snake
- Zebra

Activity

Have the animals in a pile in front of you. Teach H-I-P-P-O
to the children.

Start the song by putting the first animal on the far left
side of the felt board. As you begin each new verse, put the
next animal in line on the felt board. Sing.

After the song, talk with the children about all the pets the
child in the song had. *"What other pets could the child
have? What pets do they have?"*

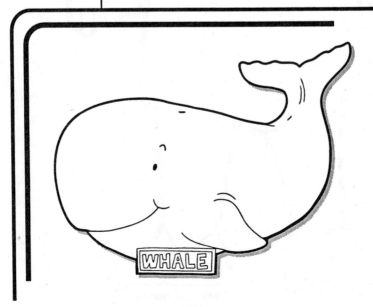

WHALE

H-I-P-P-O

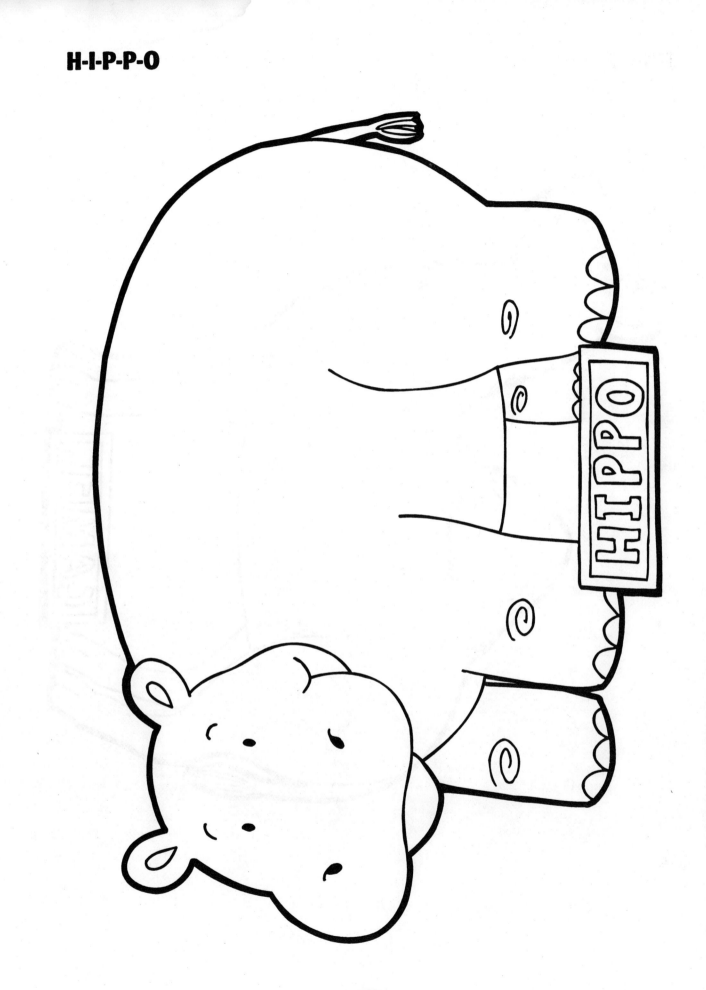

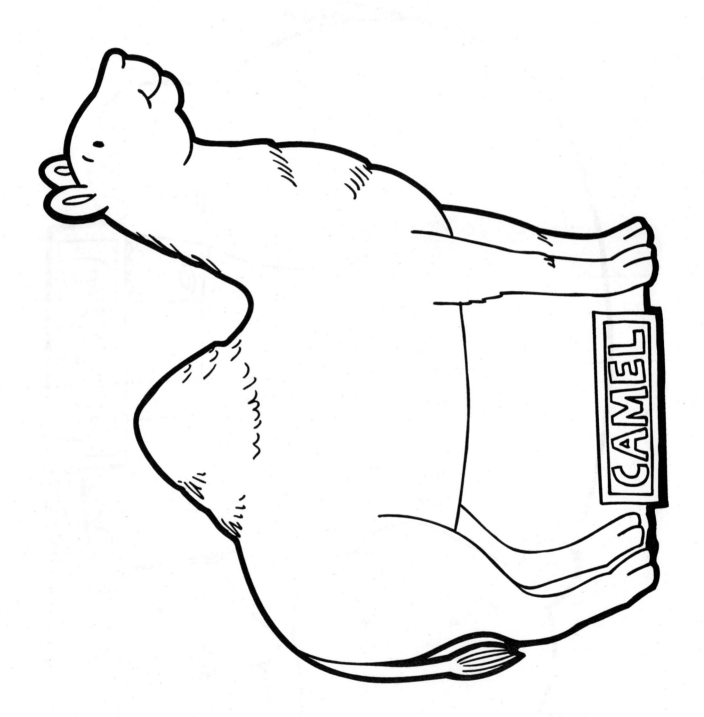

H-I-P-P-O

SNAKE

PANDA

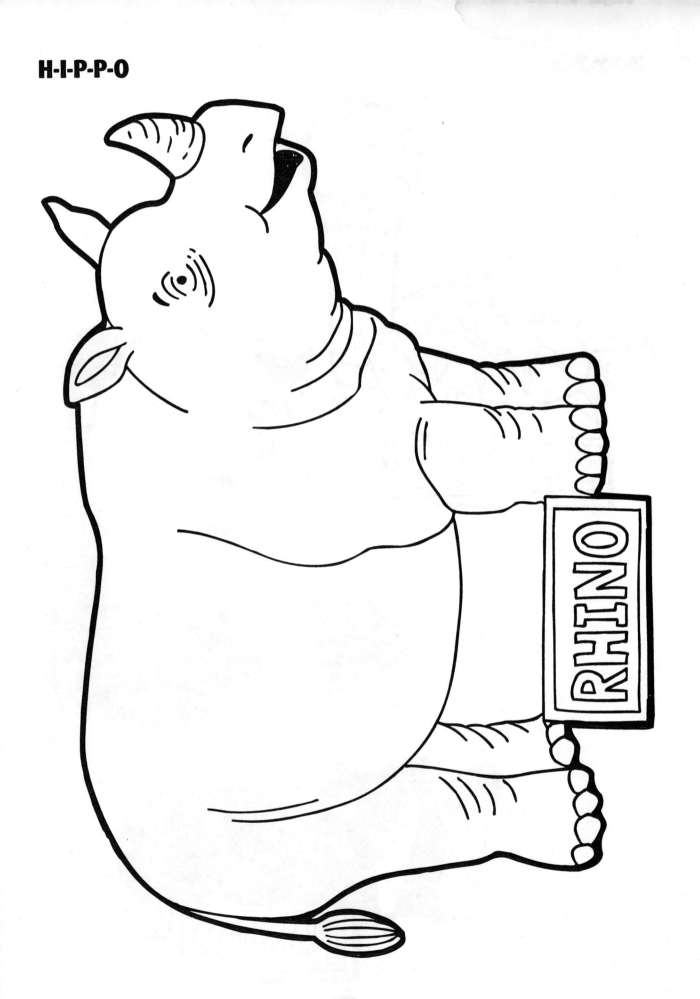

RHINO

H-I-P-P-O

H-I-P-P-O

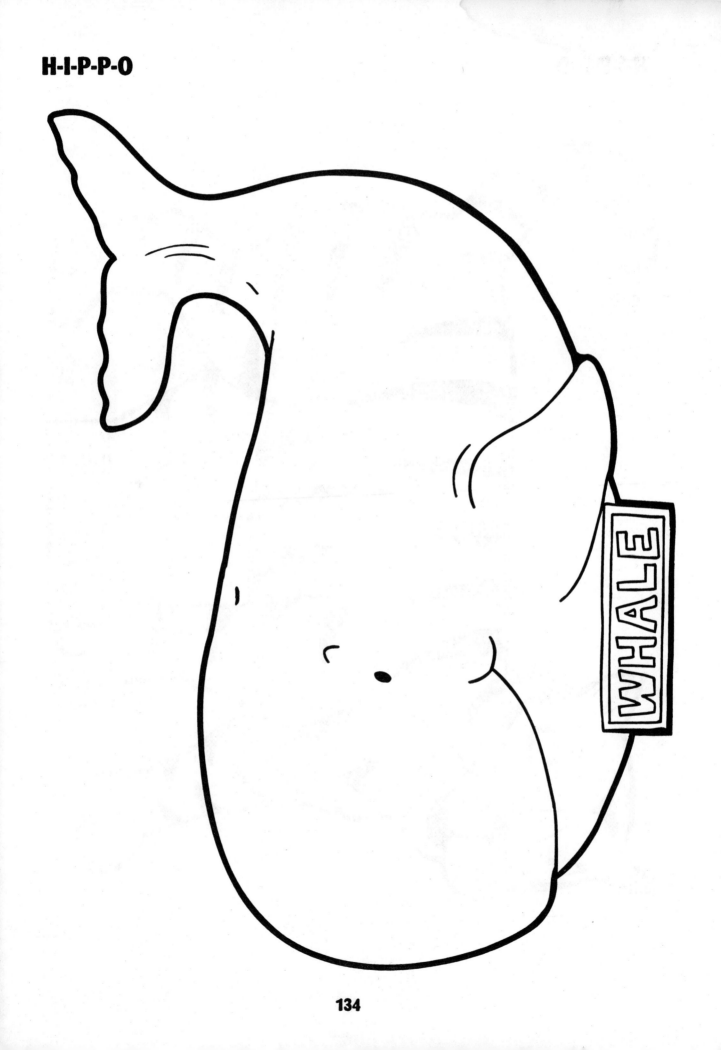

WHALE

H-I-P-P-O

Five Little Monkeys

Five little monkeys jumping on the bed.
  (Hold up five fingers.)
One fell off and bumped his head.
Mama called the doctor,
And the doctor said, *(Say firmly.)*
"No more monkeys jumping on the bed!"
  (Shake head, "no.")

Four little monkeys jumping…
Three little monkeys jumping…
Two little monkeys jumping…
One little monkey jumping…

Make

5 monkeys

Bed

Activity

Put the bed in the middle of the felt board. Have all the monkeys on the floor near you.

Tell the children that it is time for the monkeys to go to bed. Put each monkey in bed, counting with the children as you do.

After all five monkeys are in bed, start saying FIVE LITTLE MONKEYS JUMPING ON THE BED. As each monkey falls off the bed, take one and tumble her to the floor and tuck her under your leg.

Want More?

On Your Mitt – Next time put the five monkeys on your mitt, and let them tumble off each finger as you and the children chant the fingerplay.

Five Little Monkeys

Five Little Monkeys

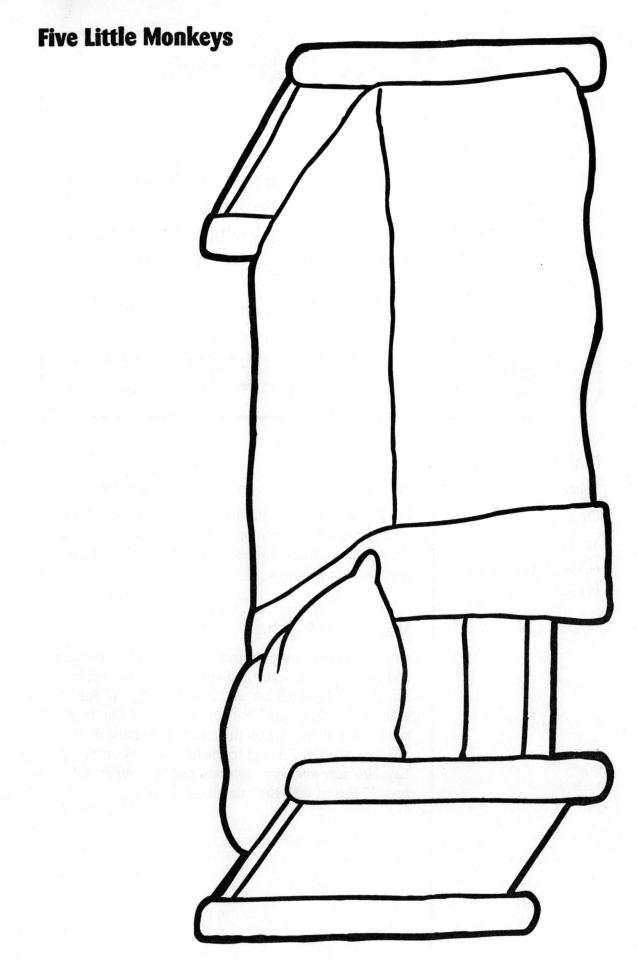

Draw a Shape

Draw a square, draw a square,
   (Draw shapes in air.)
With corners four.
Draw a square, draw a square,
Four corners, no more.

Draw a triangle, draw a triangle,
With corners three.
Draw a triangle, draw a triangle,
Three corners is all you see.

Draw a circle, draw a circle,
Make it very round.
Draw a circle, draw a circle,
No corners can be found.

Make

Square

Circle

Triangle

Optional: Three sizes
of each

Activity

Put the three felt shapes on the floor in front of you.

Say DRAW A SHAPE with the children. When you begin
each verse, put the appropriate shape on your felt board.
Point to the corners of the square and triangle and the
roundness of the circle.

Want More?

Grab a Shape – Cut out three sizes of squares, triangles,
and circles. Mix them up and put them on your felt board.
Name a child and tell her which shape to "grab." For
example say, *"Eric, grab the largest square."* Continue
until all the shapes are off the board. Then have all the
children pass their shapes to the left *(in one direction).*
Say, *"All those who have squares, put them on the felt
board."* Repeat with the triangles and circles.

Draw a Shape

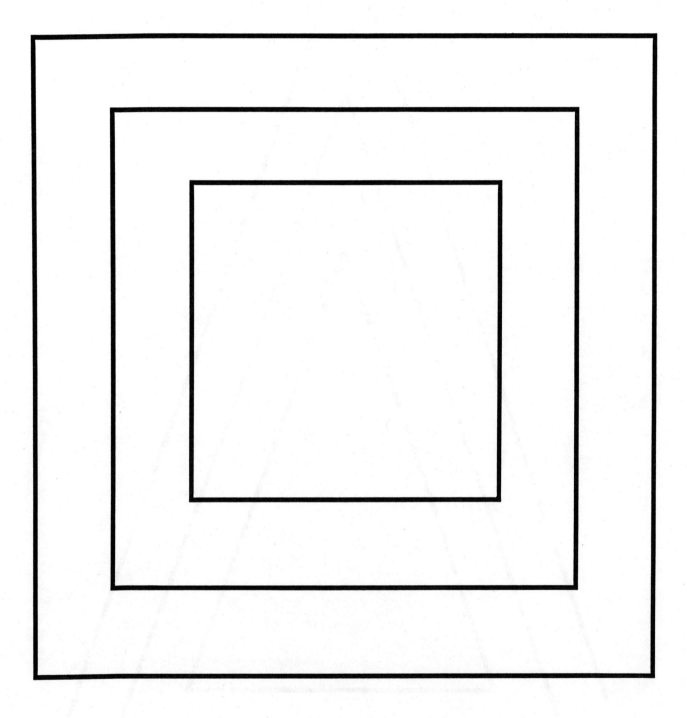

Draw a Shape

Draw a Shape

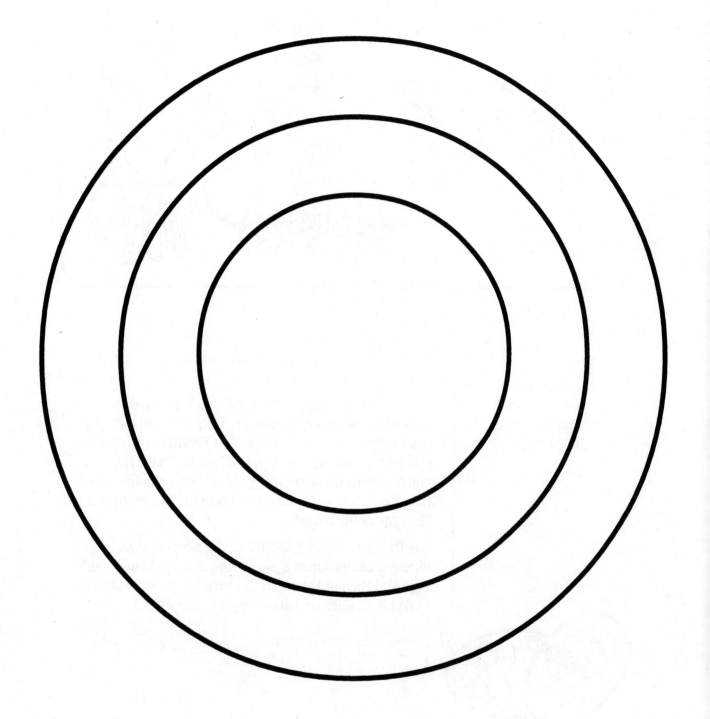

In My Easter Basket

Red eggs, yellow eggs
Green eggs too.
So many colors
I'll share some with you.
   (Point to a friend.)

by Dick Wilmes

Make

Easter basket

2 red, yellow, green, blue, purple, brown, black, orange, white, gray, pink eggs

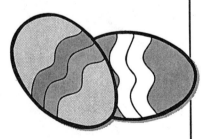

Activity

Put the Easter basket on the felt board. Have the pairs of eggs in front of you on the floor.

Pass out pairs of eggs to half the children. Have each child with a pair of eggs hold hers up. Everyone call out what color they are. Say IN MY EASTER BASKET with the children. As you say *"red, yellow, green,"* have the children with those color eggs share with children who have none. The children come up to the felt board and put the eggs in the basket.

Say IN MY EASTER BASKET again, naming three different colors. Once again let the children share their eggs and then put them in the basket. Continue until the basket is all filled up with colored Easter eggs.

In My Easter Basket

Bunny Hop

(tune: Here We Go Round the Mulberry Bush)

This is the way the bunny hops,
Bunny hops, bunny hops.
This is the way the bunny hops,
On a sunny morning.

This is the way the bunny runs...
    crawls... skates... wiggles...
    tiptoes...waves...

This is the way the bunny rests,
Bunny rests, bunny rests.
This is the way the bunny rests,
On a sunny day.

Make

Bunny face

"Action" whiskers
(Duplicate each
whisker and back with
felt.)

Activity

Put the bunny face on the felt board. Have the whiskers in front of you on the floor.

Keep the hopping and resting whiskers. Pass out the other whiskers to the children. Have each child tell the others what his bunny is doing.

Everyone stand up. Put your "hopping" whisker on the bunny's face. Everyone hop and sing BUNNY HOP. At the end of the first verse, have a child put his whisker on the bunny. Do the movement while everyone sings again. Continue until the bunny has a face full of whiskers. Put the "resting" whisker on the bunny's face last. Everyone lie down and quietly sing the last verse.

Bunny Hop

Bunny Hop

Crawl

Fly

Jump

March

Bunny Hop

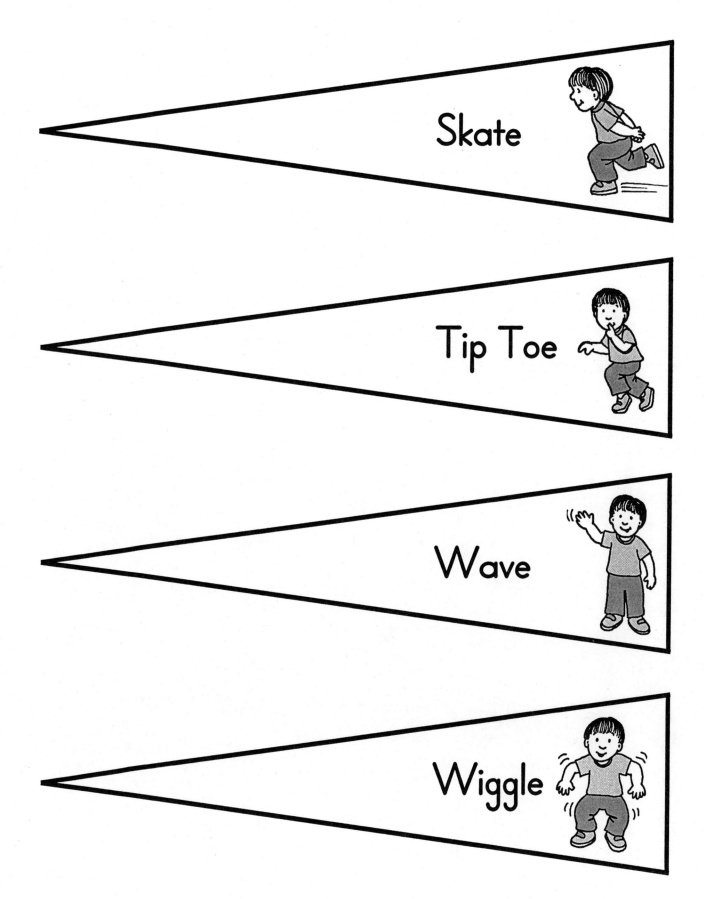

Summer Fingerplays

Clouds

(traditional rhyme adapted)

What's fluffy white and floats up high,
Like piles of ice cream in the sky?
When I look up in the big blue sky,
I see lots of things floating by.

Make

Cloud shapes

Prop

Piece of cloth to cover the felt board

Activity

Tack or tape the piece of cloth to the top of the felt board. Flip it to the backside of the feltboard. Put three or four clouds in the "sky." Cover them with the cloth. Have the rest of the clouds on the floor in front of you.

Say CLOUDS with the children. Slowly lift the fabric off the clouds. Say to the children, *"Look at all the clouds. What do you see?"* Point to each cloud and have the children call out what it reminds them of. Encourage them to think beyond the most obvious answer. Turn the cloud a different way. Does that inspire more thought? Cover up the cloud shapes.

Secretively add one or two more clouds so the children cannot see what you have added. Say CLOUDS again. Lift the fabric and have the children look at all the clouds. Say, *"There are more clouds in the sky. What's new?"* Talk about them. *"Do the old clouds remind you of anything else?"* Repeat one or two more times, until all the clouds are in the sky.

Clouds

Clouds

Clouds

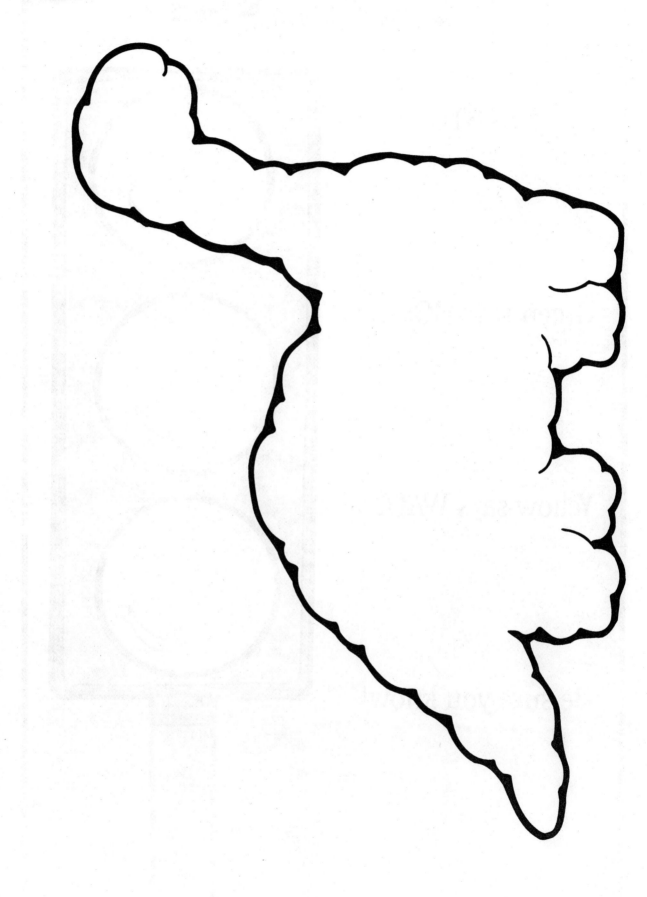

Red Says Stop

Red says STOP.

Green says GO.

Yellow says WAIT.

Be sure you know!

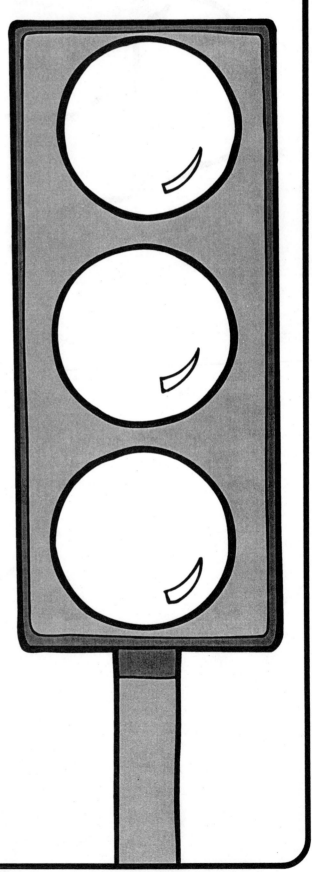

Make

Red circle

Green circle

Yellow circle

(See page 143 for the large circle pattern.)

Activity

Stand your felt board the long way. Put the three circles on the floor in front of you.

Say to the children, *"I'm going to tell you a safety riddle. I want you watch the felt board and listen to what I say. When I'm done, call out what you think I am riddling about."* Slowly say the rhyme to the children putting the three circles in order on the felt board. When you have finished, let the children call out what they think you riddled about. Talk about their response/s. Clap for the children's efforts. Take down the three circles and repeat the rhyme with them.

Want More?

Look Both Ways

Stop at the corner,
Wait for the light,
Look to the left,
Look to the right.

If nothing is coming,
Then start to walk.
Go straight across the street,
Be careful and don't talk.

Stop, Look and Listen

Stop, look, and listen
Before you cross the street.
Use your eyes and ears,
Then use your feet.

On a Picnic We Will Go

(tune: Farmer In the Dell)

On a picnic we will go.
On a picnic we will go.
Let's fill our basket up.
   (Put basket in middle of group.)
On a picnic we will go.

(Child's name) brings a blanket. *(Child skips to basket and puts
   real/pretend "blanket" in.)*
(Child's name) brings a blanket. *(Child skips back to group.)*
Let's fill our basket up.
On a picnic we will go.
Continue with other children and picnic items.
   by Liz Wilmes

Make

Large picnic basket
Beach ball
Picnic foods
- Corn
- Apples
- Grapes
- Watermelon
- Cheese
- Pop
- Chicken
- Hot dogs
- Hamburgers
- Taco
- Sandwich
- Chips
- Mustard
- Pickles
- Ketchup
- Plates
- Silverware
- Napkins
- Cups
- Cupcake

Activity

Put the picnic basket on the felt board. Pass out the picnic pieces to the children.

Tell the children that they are going on a pretend picnic, but first they must fill their basket.

Have the children stand up and hold hands. (Keeping picnic pieces.) Teach them ON A PICNIC WE WILL GO. As they sing the first verse have them walk around in a circle. Stop. Call on a child to add his picnic piece to the basket. As he does, have the group sing the second verse. Continue, always changing the verse to match the new child and his object.

Want More?

Snack Time – If the weather is nice, have an outdoor picnic snack on the playground. If the weather is not cooperating, put the picnic blanket on the floor in your room and have an indoor picnic snack.

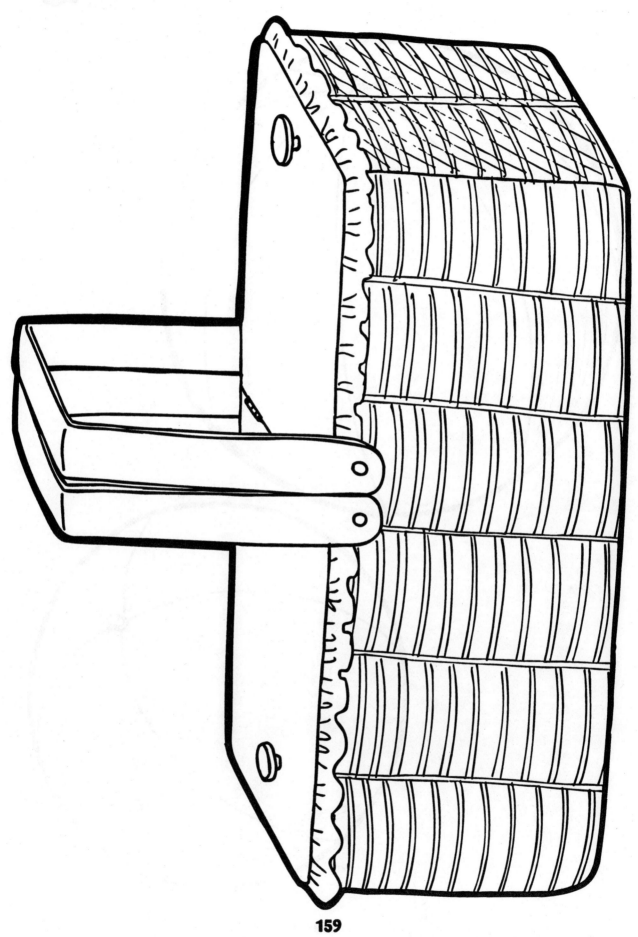

On a Picnic We Will Go

On a Picnic We Will Go

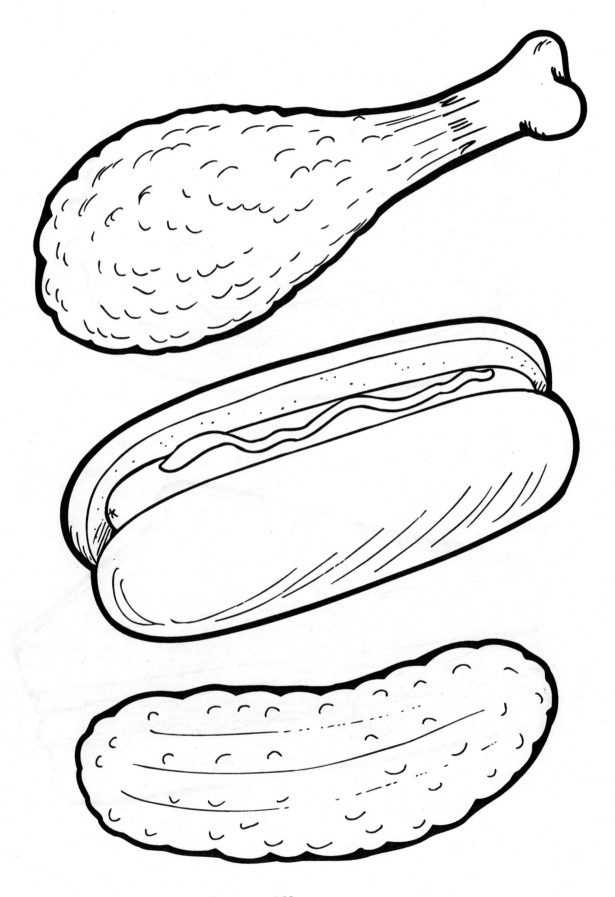

Zoo Noises

I'm a bear – hear me growl! *(Talk like a bear.)*
I'm a lion – hear me roar! *(Talk like a lion.)*
I'm a snake – hear me hiss! *(Talk like a snake.)*
I'm a zebra – hear me neigh! *(Talk like a zebra.)*
I'm an elephant – hear me grunt!
    (Talk like an elephant.)
I'm a monkey – hear me squeak! *(Talk like a monkey.)*
I'm a giraffe – I don't make a sound!
    (Talk like a giraffe.)
I'm really a child – Hear me laugh!! *(Laugh.)*

Make

Bear

Lion

Snake

Zebra

Elephant

Monkey

Giraffe

Girl and boy

Large yellow circle
(See page 143 for the large circle pattern.)

Activity

Put all the zoo animals in a row on your felt board. Put the yellow circle towards the top of your felt board off to one side.

Say to the children, *"Let's pretend that we are the animals at the zoo."* Name a child and ask her what type of zoo animal she would like to be. She says, *"I'm a _____. Hear me _____."* (Put that animal in the yellow circle.) She goes into an open space and pretends to be that animal as everyone else makes the animal's noise. After a short time, that child goes to another child and says, *"What animal are you?"* The child looks at the animals on the felt board and says, *"I'm a _____. Hear me _____."* (Switch animals in the yellow circle.) Continue until all the children have had an opportunity to be a zoo animal.

At the end, bring out the two felt children and put them on the felt board. Everyone say together, *"We are really children. Hear us laugh."*

Zoo Noises

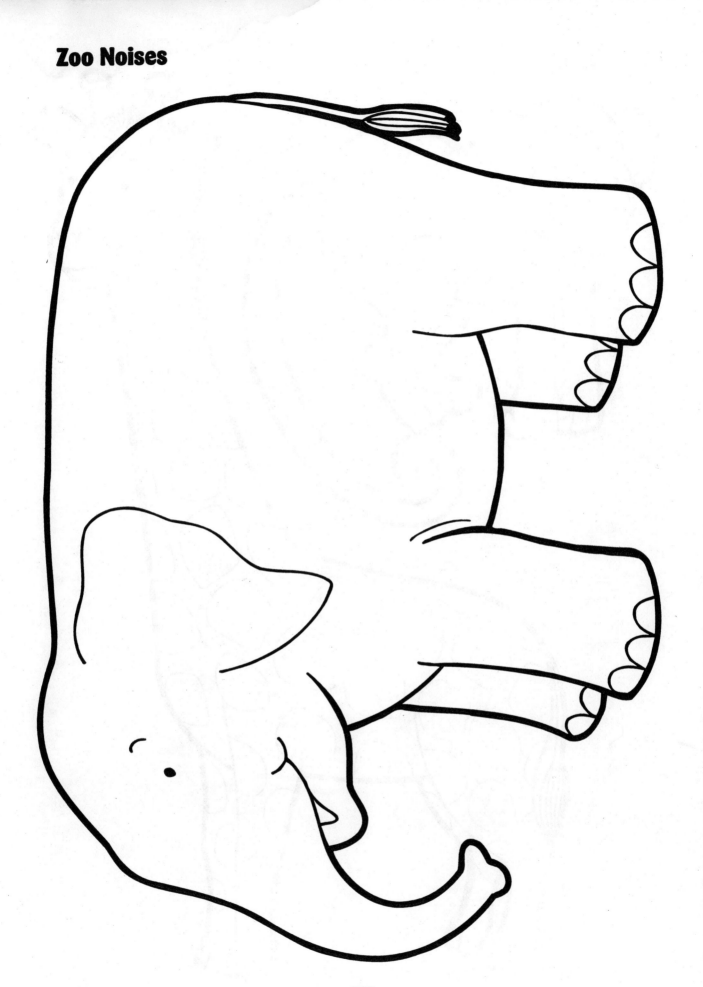

Zoo Noises

Zoo Noises

1, 2, 3 There's a Bug On Me

1, 2, 3 there's a bug on me
  (Quietly put bug someplace on you.)
Where did he go?
I don't know.
  (Shrug shoulders.)

Make

Child

Ladybug

Activity

Put the child on the felt board. Have the ladybug nearby.

Put the ladybug someplace on the felt child, such as on her shoulder, arm, knee, or head. Have the children say 1, 2, 3 THERE'S A BUG ON ME. After they say *"Where did he go? I don't know"* have them cover their eyes. You move the bug to another place on the felt child, such as under her foot, next to her shirt, etc. Open their eyes and call out where the bug is. Repeat where it is, accenting the position word. For example, *"That's where the ladybug went – on the child's knee."* Play again and again.

1,2,3, There's a Bug On Me

Shadows

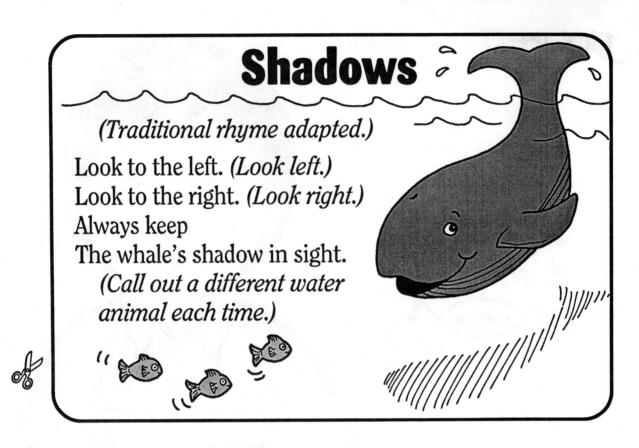

(Traditional rhyme adapted.)

Look to the left. *(Look left.)*
Look to the right. *(Look right.)*
Always keep
The whale's shadow in sight.
*(Call out a different water
animal each time.)*

Make

Black shadow of a

- Whale
- Shark
- Octopus
- Alligator
- Snake
- Frog
- Fish

Activity

Have all the felt pieces in a pile on the floor in front of you.

Put one "shadow" in the middle of the felt board. Touch the shadow on the left side and begin to say the rhyme with the children. As you continue, move your hand to the right, encouraging the children to really look at the shadow. As they say the last line, take your hand away and name the shadow as you finish.

Shadows

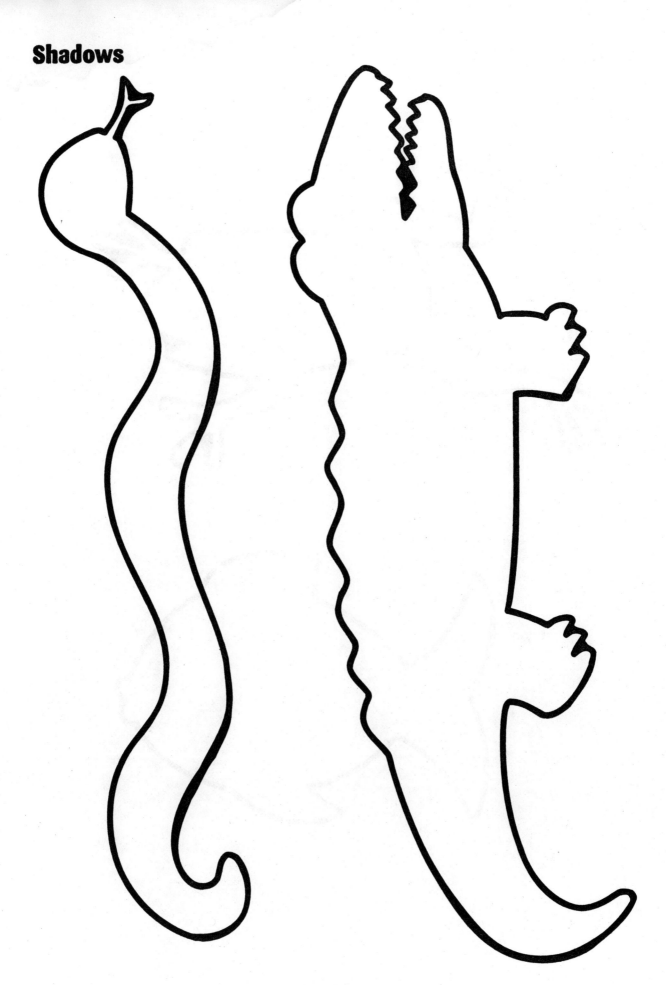

Shadows

Shadows

Five Little Monkeys Swinging In the Tree

Five little monkeys swinging in the tree.
(*Hold up five fingers.*)
Teasing Mr. Alligator, (*Swing fingers back and forth.*)
"Can't catch me!"
"Can't catch me!"
Along came Mr. Alligator (*Slow, whisper voice.*)
As quietly as can be
SNAP! (*Clap hands loudly.*)

Four little monkeys swinging…
Three little monkeys swinging…
Two little monkeys swinging…
One little monkey swinging…

Make

5 monkeys

Tree

Alligator

Activity

Put the tree in the middle of your felt board. Let the children hang the five monkeys from the tree. Put the alligator in the "water" away from the tree.

Tell the children to look at the felt board. What fingerplay do they think they're going to say? As soon as they call out FIVE LITTLE MONKEYS SWINGING FROM THE TREE, begin to say it. When you get to the second verse, slowly "swim" the alligator towards the tree. When he gets there, have the children clap their hands loudly. Jump one monkey off the tree and stick it partially behind the tree. (*He can peak out to see if any of his friends get caught.*)

Move the alligator away from the tree and repeat the fingerplay with *"Four little monkeys…"*. Continue until all the monkeys have escaped the alligator's very loud SNAPS!!

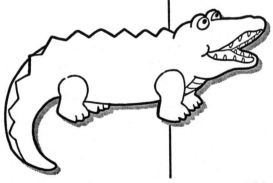

Five Little Monkeys Swinging In The Tree

Five Little Monkeys Swinging In The Tree

Five Green Bottles

There are five green bottles a-standing on the wall.
   (Hold up five fingers.)
Five green bottles a-standing on the wall.
But if one of those bottles should
   happen to fall – CRASH
There'd be four green bottles
   a-standing on the wall.

Contributed by Cheryl Airhart

Make

5 green bottles

Activity

Put five green bottles in a row near the top of your felt board. Count the bottles with the children. Then begin slowly chanting FIVE GREEN BOTTLES. When you get to the second line, hold onto one of the bottles and pull it off the wall as you chant. Put it on the floor. Sing the third line stopping before you say the number. Then everyone "shout" how many are left. Count the four bottles and then chant again in the same manner. Continue until all the green bottles have fallen off the wall.

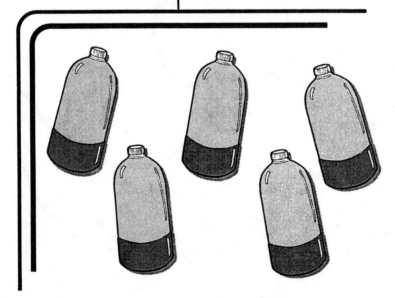

Five Green Bottles

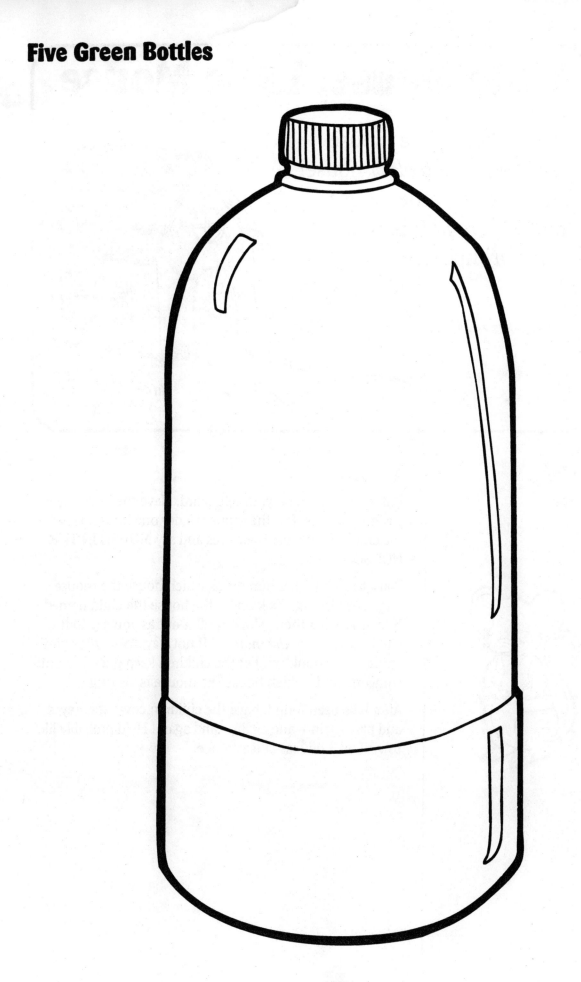

Little Mouse, Little Mouse

Little mouse, little mouse
Are you in the *(color)* house?
Little mouse, little mouse
You are *(are not)* in the
    (color) house.

Make

Mouse

8 different colored houses

Activity

Put the 8 houses on your felt board. Have the children cover their eyes. Put the mouse under one house. Have the children uncover their eyes and say MOUSE IN THE HOUSE.

Point to a child. Let him guess which house the mouse might be visiting. Peek under the house the child named. If the mouse is there, slowly pull it out as you say to the child, *"You found the mouse."* If not, say, *"Sorry"* as you shrug your shoulders. Let the children keep guessing until someone finds which house the mouse is visiting.

After he's been found, have the children cover their eyes and play again – and again – and again! He'd probably like to visit all 8 houses at least once.

Little Mouse, Little Mouse

Wheels On The Bus

The wheels on the bus go round and round,
Round and round, round and round.
The wheels on the bus go round and round,
All around the town.

The wipers on the bus go swish, swish, swish ...
The door on the bus goes open and shut ...
The horn on the bus goes beep, beep, beep ...
The windows on the bus go up and down ...
The babies on the bus go waa, waa, waa ...
The mommies on the bus go shh, shh, shh...

Make

Bus

Wheels

Wipers

Door

Horn

Windows

Baby

Mommy

Activity

Put the bus in the middle of the felt board. Line up the other pieces along the bottom.

Put the wheel up near the bus. As you do, start singing THE WHEELS ON THE BUS. After you finish the first verse, ask the children what they want to sing about next. Put that piece near the bus and sing. Continue until you've finished the song and all the pieces are around the bus.

SCHOOL BUS

Wheels On The Bus

Wheels On The Bus

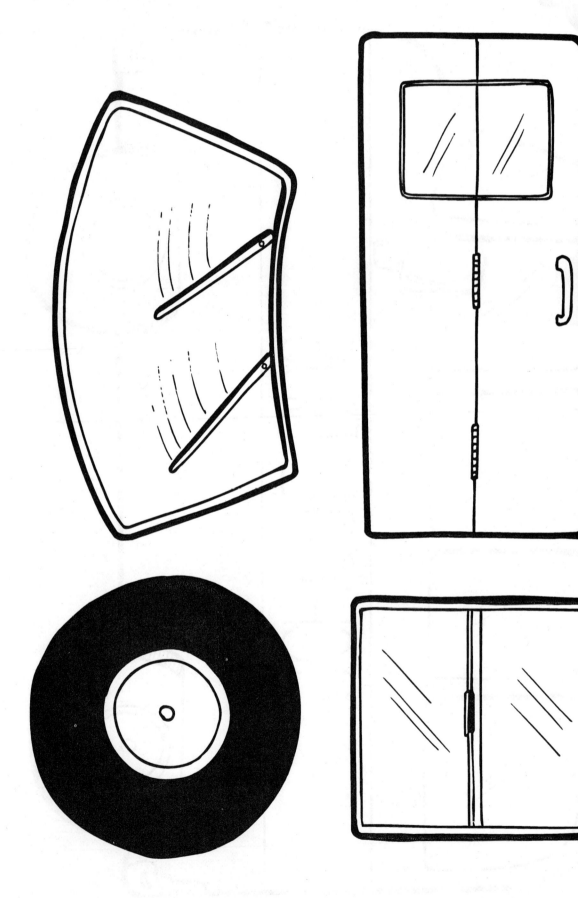

A Few More Fingerplays, Rhymes and Songs

We're Visiting the Zoo

(tune: Farmer In the Dell)

We're visiting the zoo.
We're visiting the zoo
Lions, tigers, camels, and bears.
We're visiting the zoo.

by Liz Wilmes

Use animal patterns on pages 130, 131, 133 and page 169. Change animals each time you sing.

Use Your Eyes

Use your eyes, *(Point to your eyes.)*
Use your eyes.
You can look and see.

If you're wearing
Socks *(Stop and let children look)*
Point them out to me.

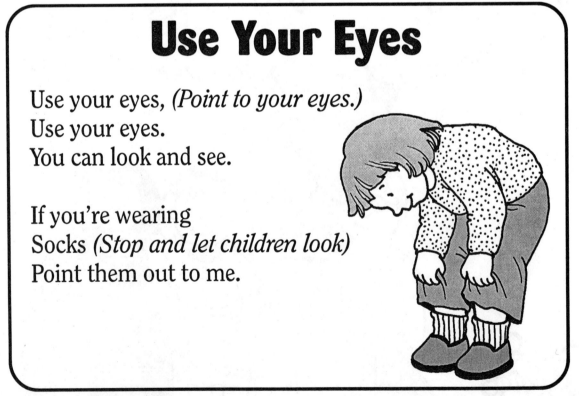

Use child pattern on pages 69, 77, 91 or 127.

My Looking Glass

I'm looking into my looking glass
    (Hold palm in front of face.)
And what kind of face do I see?

I see a happy face
Looking back at me.
    (Smile at palm of hand.)

(Change feelings and repeat.)

197

Fluttering Leaves

(tune: Farmer in the Dell)

The leaves are fluttering down *(Twirl as you sing.)*
The leaves are fluttering down
Red and yellow, orange and green
The leaves are fluttering down.

by Liz Wilmes

Use leaf patterns on pages 15-17.

We Eat Turkey

(tune: Are You Sleeping?)

We eat turkey, we eat turkey
Oh so good, oh so good

Always on Thanksgiving
Always on Thanksgiving

Yum, yum, yum,
Yum, yum, yum!

We eat...*(Let children add foods.)*

by Liz Wilmes

Johnny Works With One Hammer

Johnny works with one hammer, *(Pound 1 fist.)*
One hammer, one hammer.
Johnny works with one hammer,
Now he works with two.

Johnny works with two hammers… *(Pound 2 fists.)*
Johnny works with three hammers… *(Pound 2 fists, 1 leg.)*
Johnny works with four hammers… *(Pound with 2 fists, 2 legs.)*
Johnny works with five hammers… *(Pound 2 fists, 2 legs, head.)*

Now he goes to sleep. *(Whisper and lie down.)*

Great Big Giant Spider

The great big giant spider *(Slow, deep voice.)*
Walked up the water spout. *(Walk fingers up arm.)*
Down came the rain *(Flick fingers overhead.)*
And washed the spider out.

Out came the sun *(Big circle overhead.)*
And dried up all the rain.
And the great big giant spider
    (Walk fingers up arm.)
Walked up the spout again

Enlarge spider pattern on page 121. Use sun pattern on page 81. Create your own raindrops.

Here Is the Beehive

Here is the beehive. *(Make fist.)*
Where are the bees? *(Look at fist.)*
Hidden away where nobody sees.

Here they come creeping
Out of the hive.
1, 2, 3, 4, 5. *(Stand up fingers.)*

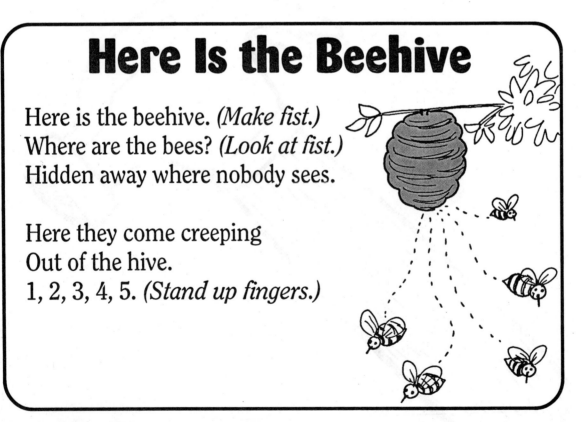

Use bee and hive patterns on page 123.

Five Little Ducks

Five little ducks that I once knew.
   (Wave 5 fingers in the air.)
Fat ones, skinny ones, tall ones too.
But the one little duck
With the feather on her back
   (Wave hands behind back.)
She led the others with a "Quack, quack, quack –
   quack, quack, quack." *(Clap hands.)*

Down the river they would go
   (Squat and waddle around.)
Wibble-wobble, wibble-wobble to and fro
But the one little duck
With the feather on her back
   (Wave hands behind back.)
She led the others with a "Quack, quack, quack –
   quack, quack, quack." *(Clap hands.)*

Up from the river they would come.
   (Continue to waddle around.)
Wibble-wobble, wibble-wobble to and fro
But the one little duck
With the feather on her back
   (Wave hands behind back.)
She led the others with a "Quack, quack, quack –
   quack, quack, quack." *(Clap hands.)*

All Of Me

See my eyes. *(Touch eyes.)*
See my nose. *(Touch nose.)*
See my chin. *(Touch chin.)*
See my toes. *(Touch toes.)*

See my waist. *(Touch waist.)*
See my knees. *(Touch knees.)*
See my arms. *(Touch arm.)*
Now you've seen all of me. *(Raise arms.)*

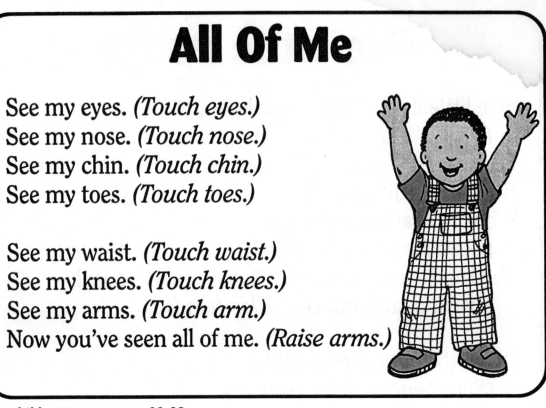

Use child pattern on page 92-93.

A Ball

Here's a ball *(Make tiny circle with fingers.)*
And here's a ball. *(Medium size ball with hands.)*
A great big ball I see. *(Large ball with arms.)*

Shall we count them?
Are you ready?
1, 2, 3.

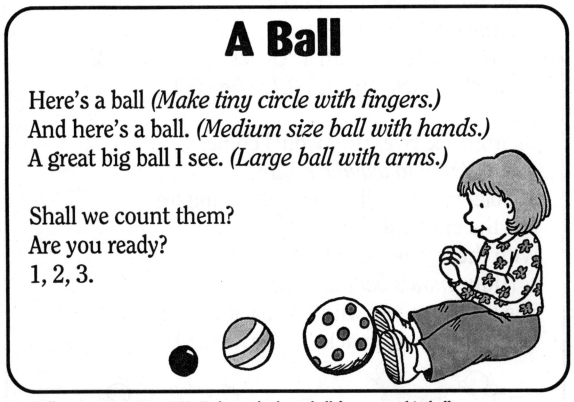

Use ball patterns on page 160. Enlarge the large ball for a great big ball.

1 Little, 2 Little, 3 Little Children

1 little, 2 little, 3 little children, *(Point at children while singing.)*
4 little, 5 little, 6 little children,
7 little, 8 little, 9 little children,
10 little boys and girls.

We hugged and we smiled and we went out to play.
   (Hug friend and smile.)
We hugged and we smiled and we went out to play.
We hugged and we smiled and we went out to play.
Ten little boys and girls.

First Lines Index

Theme Index

Animals

Alphabet

Apples

Birds

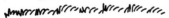

Body

Bugs and Insects

Clothes

Colors

Homes

Holidays and Seasons

Christmas

Easter

Halloween

Thanksgiving

Valentines Day

Fall

Spring

Pets

Safety

Self

Shadows

Shapes

Sky

Transportation

Weather

Work

Zoo Animals

FOR EVERY MONTH

an activity newspaper for adults
and their young children

TAKE A LOOK AT BUILDING BLOCKS NEWSPAPER

PUBLISHED:
10 times a year including an expanded summer issue.

RATES:
1 Year ~ $20^{00}
2 Years ~ $36^{50}
3 Years ~ $50^{00}
Sample ~ $ 3^{00}

SEND YOUR NAME, ADDRESS (INCLUDING ZIP CODE), AND PAYMENT TO:

BUILDING BLOCKS
38W567 Brindlewood
Elgin, Il 60123

BUILDING BLOCKS is a 20 page early childhood activity newspaper offering a total curriculum resource to use in your classroom and share with your parents.

MONTHLY FEATURES include:

~ Reproducible parent activity calendar.

~ Activity pages highlighting language, art, physical, science/math, creative, and self/social activities which are easy to plan and implement.

~ Ready-to-use charts, games, and/or posters.

~ Special activity page for toddlers and twos.

~ Large easy-to-use illustrations.

~ 4 page **FEATURED TOPIC** *Pull-Out Section.*

Library

The Circle Time Series

by Liz and Dick Wilmes. Hundreds of activities for large and small groups of children. Each book is filled with Language and Active games, Fingerplays, Songs, Stories, Snacks, and more. A great resource for every library shelf.

Circle Time Book
Captures the spirit of 39 holidays and seasons.
ISBN 0-943452-00-7   **$ 12.95**

Everyday Circle Times
Over 900 ideas. Choose from 48 topics divided into 7 sections: self-concept, basic concepts, animals, foods, science, occupations, and recreation.
ISBN 0-943452-01-5   **$16.95**

More Everyday Circle Times
Divided into the same 7 sections as EVERYDAY. Features new topics such as Birds and Pizza, plus all new ideas for some popular topics contained in EVERYDAY.
ISBN 0-943452-14-7   **$16.95**

Yearful of Circle Times
52 different topics to use weekly, by seasons, or mixed throughout the year. New Friends, Signs of Fall, Snowfolk Fun, and much more.
ISBN 0-943452-10-4   **$16.95**

Paint Without Brushes

by Liz and Dick Wilmes. Use common materials which you already have. Discover the painting possibilities in your classroom! PAINT WITHOUT BRUSHES gives your children open-ended art activities to explore paint in lots of creative ways. A valuable art resource. One you'll want to use daily.
ISBN 0-943452-15-5   **$12.95**

Easel Art

by Liz & Dick Wilmes. Let the children use easels, walls, outside fences, clip boards, and more as they enjoy the variety of art activities filling the pages of EASEL ART. A great book to expand young children's art experiences.
ISBN 0-943452-25-2   **$ 12.95**

Everyday Bulletin Boards

by Wilmes and Moehling. Features borders, murals, backgrounds, and other open-ended art to display on your bulletin boards. Plus board ideas with patterns, which teachers can make and use to enhance their curriculum.
ISBN 0-943452-09-0   **$ 12.95**

Exploring Art

by Liz and Dick Wilmes. EXPLORING ART is divided by months. Over 250 art ideas for paint, chalk, doughs, scissors, and more. Easy to set-up in your classroom.
ISBN 0-943452-05-8   **$19.95**

CIRCLE TIME

ART

Parachute Play

by Liz and Dick Wilmes. A year 'round approach to one of the most versatile pieces of large muscle equipment. Starting with basic techniques, PARACHUTE PLAY provides over 100 activities to use with your parachute.
ISBN 0-943452-03-1   **$ 9.95**

Learning Centers

by Liz and Dick Wilmes. Hundreds of open-ended activities to quickly involve and excite your children. You'll use it every time you plan and whenever you need a quick, additional activity. A must for every teacher's bookshelf.
ISBN 0-943452-13-9   **$19.95**

Play With Big Boxes

by Liz and Dick Wilmes. Children love big boxes. Turn them into boats, telephone booths, tents, and other play areas. Bring them to art and let children collage, build, and paint them. Use them in learning centers for games, walk-along vehicles, play stages, quiet spaces, puzzles, and more, more, more.
ISBN 0-943452-23-6   **$ 12.95**

Play With Small Boxes

by Liz and Dick Wilmes. Small boxes are free, fun, and provide unlimited possibilities. Use them for telephones, skates, scoops, pails, beds, buggies, and more. So many easy activities, you'll want to use small boxes every day.
ISBN 0-943452-24-4   **$ 12.95**

Felt Board Fingerplays

by Liz and Dick Wilmes. Over fifty popular fingerplays, each with full-size patterns. All accompanied by games and activities to extend the learning and play even more. Divided by seasons, this book is a quick reference for a year full of fingerplay fun.
ISBN 0-943452-26-0   **$16.95**

Felt Board Fun

by Liz and Dick Wilmes. Make your felt board come alive. Discover how versatile it is as the children become involved with a wide range of activities. This unique book has over 150 ideas with accompanying patterns.
ISBN 0-943452-02-3   **$16.95**

Table & Floor Games

by Liz and Dick Wilmes. 32 easy-to-make, fun-to-play table/floor games with accompanying patterns ready to trace or photocopy. Teach beginning concepts such as matching, counting, colors, alphabet, sorting and so on.
ISBN 0-943452-16-3   **$19.95**

Activities Unlimited

by Adler, Caton, and Cleveland. Create an enthusiasm for learning! Hundreds of innovative activities to help your children develop fine and gross motor skills, increase their language, become self-reliant, and play cooperatively. Whether you're a beginning teacher or a veteran, this book will quickly become one of your favorites.
ISBN 0-943452-17-1   **$16.95**